D1454759

Modern Day CEOs
The Good, The Bad, and The Ugly

Michael E. Heberling, Ph.D.

Peggy M. Houghton, Ph.D.

Baker College

Flint, Michigan

© **2002 by Michael E. Heberling and Peggy M. Houghton**

ISBN: 0-923568-50-6

For Further Information, Please Contact:
Baker College Center for Graduate Studies
1116 W. Bristol Rd.
Flint, MI 48507
800-469-3165

Library of Congress Cataloging-in-Publication Data

Heberling, Michael.
 Modern day CEOs : the good, the bad, and the ugly / Michael Heberling
and Peggy M. Houghton.
    p. cm.
Includes bibliographical references (p.) and index.
 ISBN 0-923568-50-6
 1. Chief executive officers--United States--Biography. 2. Success in business--United States. I. Houghton, Peggy M. II. Title.

HC102.5.A2 H43 2002
338.7'092'273--dc21
                2002013797

Manufactured in the United States of America

From Michael:

In memory of my father-in-law, J.R. Gump, Ph.D., a very close friend for over 25 years.

From Peggy:

In memory of my brother, Patrick S. Houghton, whom I loved, respected, and admired.

Table of Contents

Preface

There are a few underlying premises of this writing that should be addressed. One of these premises is that a great leader is not some type of "super hero" who was born on a different planet or under a different star. He or she is a human being with very human strengths and weaknesses who has reached a leadership position through a combination of hard work, intelligence, perseverance, and the luck to be in the right place at the right time in history.

The second underlying premise of this writing is that leaders' personality traits are demonstrated in all aspects of their lives and not just when they are on the job. In fact, when it comes to character traits, it appears that leaders exhibit similar characteristics off the job as they demonstrate on the job. Invariably, biographies of leaders reveal that those who are forceful and dynamic at work are also forceful and dynamic at home and in social situations. Similarly, leaders who are athletically inclined like to compare the challenges of their jobs to athletic events. Likewise, leaders who are risk takers at work also tend to risk takers when it comes to hobbies and outside interests.

There has been a deliberate attempt in these biographies to include information regarding each leader's personal life. This was not done to appeal to the reader's prurient interests, but to demonstrate the belief that leaders (indeed, most people) cannot effectively divorce their career from the other aspects of their life. A person who is arrogant, temperamental, and demanding at work will most likely be arrogant, temperamental, and demanding at home, which may help explain the disproportionate number of unhappy relationships and divorces which were revealed in the research.

Finally, the issue of timeliness must be considered. Active leaders who are in charge of dynamic and fast-moving companies are profiled in the writing. The men and women covered will undoubtedly move on to other challenges, and/or their respective companies may be acquired, merged, or simply forced out of business.

However, the personalities, practices and principles that put these men and women into leadership positions will still be worthy of study. And the unique personality characteristics, management techniques and work ethic of these leaders will still provide important insights into that rare, elusive and hard-to-define quality that is known as "leadership."

Jeffrey P. Bezos
Chief Executive Officer
Amazon.com

The Chronology of Jeffrey Bezos

On January 12, 1964, Jackie Gise Preston gave birth to a son whom she named Jeffrey Preston. She was only 17 years old at the time of the child's birth, and her premature marriage ended after only one year. Young Jeff's father then left the family...never to return.

Miguel Bezos, who was known to others as Mike Bezos, courted and eventually fell in love with Jackie. In 1968, Mike married Jackie, and later legally adopted her son Jeff. At the time, Jeff was four years old. Five years after Jeff's birth, his half sister Christina was born; the following year, his half brother Mark entered the Bezos family (Brackett, 2001). Today, Jeff Bezos has no recollection of his biological father, nor does he have any desire to learn about him. He has been noted as saying,

> But the reality, as far as I'm concerned, is that my dad [Mike Bezos] is my natural father. The only time I ever think about it, genuinely, is when a doctor asks me to fill out a form. It's a fine truth to have out there. I'm not embarrassed by it. (cited in Spector, 2000, p. 3)

Spector (2000) further notes that Bezos was precocious as an adolescent…willful, focused, and confident. He was active as well as popular throughout his high school years. He was determined, intelligent, and driven toward success. As a leader on the football field, he not only remembered his own assignment, but the assignments of all the other team members as well.

Bezos was accepted to Princeton in the fall of 1982. He graduated summa cum laude in 1986 with a B.S.E. in electrical engineering and computer science. His grade point average in his department was a 4.2 out of 4.0 (Princeton gives a 4.3 for an A+); his overall grade point average was 3.9 (Spector, 2000).

Upon graduation, Jeff Bezos accepted a position with a financial services company. After two years of an intense learning experience, he decided it was time to broaden his horizons. He eventually landed a job at D. E. Shaw & Co., a company considered to be the most cutting-edge trading firm on Wall Street. Bezos sought, and was given, an extraordinary amount of responsibility for a person his age. He soon became well-versed in computer protocols and communications networks. He managed a department dealing with Fortune 500 clients, where he dealt with billions of dollars of cash and assets and gained invaluable experience in international expansion. From this experience, he developed the following leadership precepts (Spector, 2000):

- Be extraordinarily selective in hiring.

- Hire people who are open, creative and able to think for themselves.

- Be a leader by articulating excitement about the business. Likewise, be able to convey that excitement to the employees.

- Find a business where there is no perceived leader and/or where the barriers for entry are low.

- Offer a product or service that is easily understandable.

- Follow your heart. If you feel you will one day regret not taking a chance, then take that chance. Bezos calls this "regret-minimization." (Spector, 2000, p. 32).

After a few successful years at D. E. Shaw's firm, Bezos' intellectual curiosity needed to be stimulated once again. He began to research Internet technology. After much study, he recommended to David Shaw that D. E. Shaw should consider selling books on the Internet. The idea was not well received by the company's principals. In fact, it was flat out rejected. But Bezos is the type of person who simply would not accept no for an answer. He resigned from his position, and began his own Internet bookselling company.

> I knew that when I was eighty there was no chance that I would regret having walked away from my 1994 Wall Street bonus in the middle of the year. I wouldn't even have remembered that. But I did think there was a chance that I might regret significantly not participating in this thing called the Internet, that I believed passionately in. I also know that if I had tried and failed, I wouldn't regret that. (Bezos, as cited in Spector, 2000, p. 31)

Amazon.com…the Bezos Way

Bezos left the financial freedom and job security that he had gained as a respected Vice-President of the Wall Street firm D. E. Shaw in 1994. He moved to Seattle, Washington, and began to develop a business plan for his company, which would ultimately be called Amazon.com. Throughout his extensive research at D. E. Shaw, he had learned that the annual Web growth was projected at 2,300 percent.

He believed in this optimistic projection and came up with a list of what he considered to be the five most viable products to be sold over the Internet. These products included compact discs, computer hardware, computer software, videos, and books. He finally narrowed his business to the sale of books over the Web. This was due primarily to the large worldwide market for literature, the low price of books, and the strong selection of titles that were available in print (Spector, 2000).

> *"I will change the economics of the book industry as a whole."*
> —Jeff Bezos

Amazon.com initially operated out of Bezos' garage. It did not take long before the company grew to the point where it needed a separate building. Seattle was chosen as the company headquarters because of the city's high-tech intellectual capital. In the beginning phases of his business, Bezos worked hard to raise funds for the company, while also working with the software developers to build the company's website. His website debuted in 1995 and soon became the number one book-related site on the Web.

After just four months of operation, Amazon.com became one of the premier leaders on the World Wide Web. It earned honors as the sixth best site on Point Communications' "Top Ten" list, and was almost immediately voted into Yahoo's "What's Cool" list and Netscape's "What's New" list (Whiteley, 1999).

Customers could enter search information, prompting the system to sift through the company's million plus database, and locate desired titles. The program would then display information about the selection on a customer's computer screen and allow the customer to order the books via a credit card. The books would then be shipped within a few days.

His competition (ordinary bookstores) generally held large inventories in warehouses. Amazon.com, however, carried only a few of the most popular titles in its Seattle warehouse. The majority of orders were routed directly to wholesalers and publishers. Consequently, large warehouse facilities were not required. The company would simply order the books from conventional sources, receive them, and then re-package and re-ship them to the customer.

Going Public in 1997

Less than two years into operation, Amazon.com went public in May 1997 with an initial public offering of 3,000,000 shares of Common Stock. With the revenue, Bezos improved the website, as well as the firm's distribution capabilities (Whiteley, 1999).

Due to the high volume of orders, a new distribution center was opened in New Castle, Delaware. In addition, the Seattle center was enlarged by 70 percent. These expansions increased the company's stocking and shipping capabilities, and reduced the time required to fill orders. The new East Coast facility helped to increase orders from customers on that side of the country...plus it was in closer proximity to East Coast publishers, thus reducing the time that it took Amazon.com to order, receive and ship books (Whiteley, 1999).

Another significant growth area for Amazon.com was the success of its "Associates Program." This program allowed companies, individuals and special interest groups who developed their own websites to offer books of interest to the users of those sites, and make them available on those sites. People visiting these Associate sites would place book orders, which would then be sent directly to Amazon.com, and were subsequently filled. Associates received periodic reports on their sales, and were granted three to eight percent commission from the books sold on their sites (Whiteley, 1999).

In October 1997, Bezos was able to report that Amazon.com was the first Internet retailer to reach the milestone of one million customers.

> To do something a little bit crazy, you have to be very optimistic, and I was. I always expected Amazon.com to be very successful. But what's unusual is that it has vastly outpaced my expectations in terms of how big a company it has become.
>
> —Jeff Bezos

Prosperity Continues...

In 1998, Amazon.com continued to take advantage of the booming economy. The company added Amazon.com Advantage, which was a program to help the sales of independent authors and publishers. Additionally, they added Amazon.com Kids, a service providing over 100,000 titles for younger children and teenagers.

The business also expanded in 1998 through three acquisitions. Two of the companies were acquired to expand the Amazon.com empire into Europe. These companies were Bookpages and Telebook. Both companies gave Amazon.com access to new customers in Europe, as well as globally expanded the reach of existing customers. A third acquisition, Movie Database, was used to support plans for future online video sales (Whiteley, 1999).

One final change in 1998 was the announcement of the firm's decision to enter into the online music business. It eventually opened this segment of the business in June 1998, with over 125,000 available titles. The database had the capability to be searched via artist, song title, or label. Even more impressive was the fact that customers were able to listen to more than 225,000 sound clips before making their final purchase decision (Whiteley, 1999).

Throughout these years of growth and success, Amazon.com never made a profit. True to his management and leadership principles, Jeff Bezos never promised one. He concentrated on hiring good people, delivering good customer service, and looking for logical ways to expand the Amazon.com empire. He was confident that he was on the right track, and that profits would be forthcoming if he remained true to his basic business plan.

The company is losing less money every year, and it seems to have survived the dot.com fallout of 2001. It's a tribute to Jeff Bezos that investors still believe in his company and are still willing to invest in it despite the demise of hundreds of other dot.com companies.

"Ten Secrets" to Success

One of the biggest reasons so many other dot.com companies failed was the fact that their founders did not really understand the Internet and its capabilities and shortcomings. They tried to use it to market products and services that were not suitable for the media, as well as products and services that aroused the suspicions of their potential customers. Also, the large number of scams using the Internet made customers inherently leery of many legitimate offers.

The beauty of Amazon.com is that it offers products that are desirable to almost everyone, and products that are so relatively inexpensive that scam artists are not likely to try to take over. It's an idea that is beautiful in its simplicity…yet one that Jeff Bezos tends to make light of. He believes that "It's easy to come up with an idea. The hard part, however, is the actual implementation." To this end, he developed his "ten secrets" (Saunders, 1999, pp.17-19).

Secret #1: Understand E-Commerce.

Amazon's founder studied the book market before choosing it as a starting place for Amazon. More importantly, he studied and understood the Internet. He has said that this knowledge is Amazon's hard-earned advantage over barnesandnoble.com and Borders.com. Today, as he faces competition from eBay and other online operations, this expertise should help him stay a step ahead of his competitors.

The popularity of the World Wide Web was just beginning during the 1990s…and very few people even dreamt that the Internet would evolve into what it is today. As the use of the Web became almost necessary to survive in a competitive world, companies soon considered the Web a new avenue for commerce. Selling products via the Internet allowed companies to reach virtually anyone in the world and provided companies with an opportunity to compete globally.

Secret #2: Build an Entrepreneurial Team.

Bezos has brought together a talented and diverse group of people. He has given them a challenge: to change the world in a fundamental way by making Amazon a success. He has also given them a sense of ownership of that mission, through generous stock-option incentives.

> *"You can work long, hard, and well.*
> *At Amazon.com, two out of three won't work."*
> —Jeff Bezos

From the infancy stages of his company, Bezos has looked for the following characteristics in people while conducting interviews:

Intense, hard-working, smart people, who are secure enough to hire other great people. When I interview somebody, I spend about a third of the interview asking them questions designed to ascertain whether or not they can hire great people. It's sort of a 'meta-interview.' (Spector, 2000, pp. 107-108)

He once told the *Wall Street Journal* that managers who lack the confidence to hire stellar performers "Have to understand that if they don't hire them, they'll be working for them down the road."

He wanted to attract people who had a talent or quality—unrelated to the job—such as music or athletics, which would add a dimension to their value because, "When you are working very hard and very long hours, you want to be around people who are interesting and fun to be with" (Spector, 2000, p. 157).

Secret #3: Focus.

Bezos has articulated a mission, but he isn't only talking about that. His actions exhibit a clarity of purpose that is allowing his young company to stay grounded as it goes through the turbulent transitions of growth, and meets competitors head on. Bezos knows that there are many smaller issues that arise that can distract from that main goal, and he has had to focus on those things that count most.

Spector (2000) notes that if an organization is to achieve its long-term goals, it needs to abide by a strategic planning process. Specifically, the process includes the following:

- Clarity of your purpose. Whether an organization is on the Web or made from bricks and mortar, its leader must first define the nature of the business. In short, the CEO and top management team needs to answer the simple question, "Why are we here?"

- Know where you are going. After all, you cannot get there unless you have some idea where you want to be five or ten years from now. Ideally, the long-term viewpoint should cascade down as short-term plans are made for the business.

- Ask where are you now. Most established businesses constantly analyze their market strengths and weaknesses. But even relatively young businesses should ask themselves about strengths, weaknesses, opportunities, and challenges. A key point in reviewing challenges is to remember that they can be opportunities if viewed from a different perspective.

- Practice strategic planning. The group as a whole should identify the three most important areas of the business in which to excel in order to ensure overall corporate success.

- Develop core outcomes. Just as you have identified the mission, nature of the business, and long-term objectives, you have to identify short-term or nearer-term goals for the business (usually over a 12-month period). These must be consistent with the purpose and the CEO's vision for the company.

- Develop strategies for each outcome. Strategies are different from tactics, which is the last step. Tactics are the step-by-step actions to be taken to achieve each strategy. Strategies are broader game plans for achieving each of the three outcomes identified. In the case of Amazon.com, those outcomes were likely "shop-tainment," "innovation," and "delivery."

- Develop tactics. These are the specific, measurable action plans—including the name of the person to be held responsible—tied to the strategies. (pp. 74-75)

Secret #4: Brand the Site.

From the name he gave his site, to his deals with other heavily trafficked websites that would channel users to his site, Bezos demonstrates how important branding is to e-commerce.

"It's very important, when planning a business, to look at what is the brand promise that you're going to make to customers," said Bezos. "And the brand promise that you make has to actually coincide very, very closely with the things that you can deliver. That's an important, but sometimes overlooked, component" (Spector, 2000, pp. 121-122).

Bezos and his colleagues decided that simplicity would be the company brand. They wanted to demonstrate and offer something that a typical consumer could comprehend.

> Brands to a certain degree are like quick-drying cement. When they're young, they're stretchable and pliant, but over time they become more and more associated with a particular thing and harder to stretch. (Bezos, as cited in Saunders, 1999, p. 92)

Secret #5: Get and Keep Customers by Offering Value.

This means not only a discount on price, but a rich selection, customer retention through customized service, and fun. Bezos believes that you can offer price discounts, you can offer easy-to-use search and browse features, you can provide e-mail services, and you can secure Web-based credit card payment, but customers also want speedy delivery of their purchases.

Jeff Bezos was obsessed with customer service. He often said that he wanted to make Amazon.com "the most customer-centric" company in the world (Spector, 2000, p. 126). He was an advocate of positive word-of-mouth and felt that this type of advertising had more of an impact on consumer perception than did any other form of paid advertisement. He noted, "It was seeing how successful word-of-mouth was in that first year that really led us on this path of being obsessively, compulsively, anal-retentively focused on customer service" (Spector, 2000, p. 126).

Word-of-mouth is a form of advertising that apparently is even more important online than it is within the confines of brick-and-mortar retailers. Bezos continuously reiterated the significance of this advertising technique to his employees. He explained that, in the real world, if you make a customer unhappy he or she might tell 5 or 10 friends. However, in the virtual world, if you make a customer unhappy, he or she had the capability to potentially tell 50,000 friends! (Spector, 2000).

Secret #6: Set Up a Distribution Network.

Bezos has opened four state-of-the-art distribution centers to shorten order-to-mailbox time for Amazon customers everywhere. Michael Porter talks about value chains for competitive advantage, and the Amazon.com chain includes not only use of the Internet as a sales channel, but mastery of distribution channels to be able to better serve customers.

Total Quality Management (TQM) was the buzzword of the 1980s. Businesses globally attempted to practice the concept within their everyday operations. As of late, however, terms such as "autonomous work teams" and "empowerment" seem to be more in vogue. As Spector (2001) points out, however, TQM is still the relevant concept with regard to Amazon's distribution network. It is Bezos' objective to "offer the right product in the right location at the right time with the right packaging in the right quantity at a reasonable price to the right customer" (p. 123).

Secret #7: Practice Frugality.

Bezos runs a tight ship. He recognizes that by watching his overhead, he can spend much more on business expansion, which in e-commerce translates into more customers for his site.

Bezos is well aware that lean companies are better able to change and be as innovative as the market demands. Lean management does not have to equate with mean management. Working for an organization that is bottom-line oriented can be just as, if not more, rewarding than working in a more bureaucratic environment.

Secret #8: Practice Technoleverage.

Amazon's brick-and-mortar competitors used superior inventory and ordering technology to overwhelm smaller retailers. Amazon is now rattling these giant booksellers and other retailers with its online book reviewing and ordering system, as well as other recently purchased technology. A good example is its ownership of Junglee Corporation's search engine, which permits online comparison shopping.

Being a technology leader means being cutting edge. Bezos believes in being the best in the industry. In an effort to be the best, Amazon.com adheres to the following philosophies:

- Conduct technology assessments to identify technological needs of the market and organization.

- Be willing to invest in new technology. It's cheaper and faster to buy ready-made software.

- Always set the example. If you are to get into the business of running a website, then you want your site to be the one to which customers compare existing and new businesses.

- Conduct frequent technology audits to determine how your site stands up to competitors.

- Acquire proprietary technology.

- Overcome technological shortcomings. Give visitors to your site reason to wait for the site to boot up, like interesting editorial content or fun ways to get involved.

- Be flexible in your strategy. Technoleverage requires not only maximizing the newest technology available, but also adapting, where appropriate, organizational plans and strategies, as well as processes, to reflect the technological changes.

Secret #9: Constantly Reinvent Oneself.

Enlightened imitation is necessary for Internet success. The rivalry between Amazon.com, the current leader, and barnesandnoble.com demonstrates the necessity of constant reinvention to achieve success. As Barnes and Noble launches television and advertising campaigns and duplicates Amazon's earlier tactics to draw customers to its site, Amazon has had to take countermeasures. These include expanding its offerings and acquiring technology companies like Junglee and PlanetAll—and more recently its purchase of DrugStore.com and an online pet supply store and supermarket. While extension of its product line has meant new competitors, it has also added reasons for customers to visit the site—which is necessary for the eventual profitability of Amazon.

The futurist, Joel Barker, argues that, "Today's success guarantees nothing for the future" (Barker, 1989). Jeffrey Bezos would wholeheartedly agree with this statement. His belief appears to be that if a company remains stagnant, regardless of its history of success, it is destined for failure. Consequently, being innovative and "thinking outside of the box" is required of any employee under Bezos' leadership.

Secret #10: Grow by Strategic Alliances as well as Acquisitions.

One year after launch, Amazon pioneered the concept of syndicated selling. Today it is linked with more than 60,000 sites, including five of the top six sites on the Web—AOL.com, Yahoo!, Netscape, GeoCities, and Excite. Visitors to all of these sites can purchase books from the Amazon.com catalog. Other deals have enabled Amazon to grow globally, expand its sales beyond books, differentiate itself from others online and off, and position itself for further growth.

The traditional best way to grow a business is by doing a good job for current customers, and by having those customers tell others about your business. But Spector (2000) contends that there are six other, non-traditional, ways that a business can be expanded. These are:

- Joint ventures. These arrangements allow two or more businesses to pool their resources for a common gain.

- Strategic alliances. Companies can choose to form strategic alliances to investigate technology, reduce individual expenses, expand globally, explore new marketing opportunities, increase distribution channels or improve supply chain management.

- Investments. Larger companies can purchase minority positions in smaller businesses, or they can provide venture capital for a business start-up.

- Licensing. An enterprise may license another business to use a patent or a proprietary product or process. In return, it receives royalties from the license.

- Market agreements. Such agreements can help companies widen the distribution of their products at least cost.

- Technology agreements. The high cost of technology development has prompted companies to share their knowledge and development costs.

It's interesting that Jeff Bezos has employed most of these strategies in directing Amazon.com to its amazing growth record. Mr. Bezos deserves credit for realizing that, while the Internet was an exciting and brand new media, many of the tools and strategies for building a successful Internet business were virtually the same tools and strategies used to build a conventional business. He successfully combined the old and the new...and the results speak for themselves.

The Company Offerings

The mission of the Amazon.com organization was initially to use the Internet to transform book buying into the fastest, easiest, and most enjoyable shopping experience possible. Although the customer base and product offerings have grown considerably since the beginning, the company still maintains the original commitment to customer satisfaction and the delivery of an educational and inspiring shopping experience.

Amazon.com has grown to become the Earth's Biggest Selection of products, including free electronic greeting cards; online auctions; and millions of books, CDs, videos, DVDs, toys, games, and electronics. This leading online shopping site has serviced over 29 million customers in more than 160 different countries. Just about anything that a client desires can be found at the company (Amazon.com, 2001).

Incorporated with the catalog products, the company offers a variety of other shopping services and partnership opportunities. Those who visit the Amazon.com website are able to do the following:

- Search for books, music, videos, and more. Only one word related to the desired product is required.

- Browse the virtual aisles in a myriad of product categories…everything from audio books, jazz, and video documentaries to coins and stamps that are up for auction.

- Get instant personalized recommendations based on prior purchases.

- Sign up for Delivers, an e-mail subscription service, to receive the latest reviews of exceptional new titles in categories of interest.

- Find 1.2 million British books in print at Amazon.co.uk, plus over 250,000 U.S. titles. Thousands of CDs, VHS, and DVD titles can also be scanned. In addition, the site hosts online auctions and includes items for sale from zShops sellers. Over 1 million books can be selected.

- Sign up for Special Occasion Reminder service.

- Become an Amazon.com Associate and earn money simply by selling products on personal web pages.

The Amazon.com family of websites also includes Internet Movie Database (www.imdb.com), the Web's comprehensive source of information on more than 250,000 movies and entertainment programs and 1 million cast and crew members dating from 1891 to the present (Amazon.com, 2001). In addition, Amazon.com has also invested in leading Internet retailers with similar values. A sampling of the retailers includes the following:

- Drugstore.com: an online retail and information source for health, beauty, wellness, personal care, and pharmacy. The site can be located at www.drugstore.com.

- Ashford.com: an online retailer of luxury and premium products offering new and vintage watches, fragrances, leather accessories, sunglasses, and writing instruments. The site can be located at www.ashford.com.

- EZiba.com: a leading online retailer of hand-crafted products from around the world. It can be located at www.eziba.com (Amazon.com, 2001).

Growth Pitfalls

Mr. Bezos' grasp of the new world of the Internet, combined with his knowledge of sound business principles, has made Amazon.com an amazing example of growth. But growth is not the complete answer to success, and it can sometimes be bittersweet. The following excerpts are taken from a recent interview with Stephen B. Shepard, and they indicate that everything hasn't been rosy for Mr. Bezos and his investors:

Mr. Shepard: *Your stock price went from $113 to a low of about $8. You're up to about $13 now. How do investors value a company like Amazon?*

Mr. Bezos: The only way that I know how to think about Amazon.com is in the very long term. The sector that we are in is highly volatile. The stock actually traded below its IPO price for a while. So you could have bought, at the time of our IPO, Amazon stock for roughly $1.25. It's up by a factor of seven or eight even today which, over three and a half years, is not a bad return. The people who bought and held from our IPO may curse themselves for not selling at $100, but this is, in many cases, their best investment ever.

I have long warned individual investors—I started doing this two years or so ago—to stay away from Amazon.com and other Internet stocks; not because of the absolute price levels, but because of the volatility. They are not individual investor stocks. They are not "sleep at night" stocks.

Mr. Shepard: *What have you learned from the dot.com crash?*

Mr. Bezos: The company is not the stock. The clearest way I can describe it is that back in the year 1999, when the stock market was booming and Amazon stock prices were booming, we had about 14 million customers buy from us in that year. In 2000, when the stock was busting, we had about 20 million customers buying from us. So if the stock is the company, somebody forgot to tell the customers.

Mr. Shepard: *Is running Amazon as much fun as it used to be?*

Mr. Bezos: The truth is yes. Sure I like being the poster child...but I'm a change junkie. I love the rate of change. I love the intellectual challenge of what we're doing. I love the people I work with. It's not like me against the world. We've got a big team of people. It's fun ("The Company," 2001).

Although Jeff Bezos remains very evasive about predictions as to when the company will become profitable, he recently revealed an internal e-mail that was sent out to 7,000 Amazon.com employees.

> We are very much driving toward profitability. We have, for the first time, set an internal goal with the date for when the company as a whole is going to be profitable. We're putting a stake in the ground: We're going to become profitable. That's right. We're aiming to have sales of $5 billion, produce over $1 billion in gross profits, and achieve solid operating profitability by...

Bezos then blacked out the date, citing the company's policy against making forward-looking financial statements.

In its first five years of operation, Amazon.com lost a total of $1.74 billion and borrowed $2 billion. This reality forced Bezos to significantly cut spending, revamp the culture, lay people off, and hire old-economy geniuses to teach him Six Sigma and inventory management. The result was a leaner, more efficient retailer.

In the beginning the company had just one mission: to make sales grow. "Our initial strategy was very focused and very unidimensional. It was GBF: Get big fast. We put that on our shirts at the company picnic: They said GET BIG FAST, and on the back, EAT ANOTHER HOT DOG." The theory was simple: once Amazon got big enough, the efficiencies of a virtual store would kick in, and Amazon would be in the black (Brooker, 2000).

Is There a Future for Amazon?

Jeffrey Bezos is the eternal optimist. He told Katrina Brooker of *Fortune Magazine* (2000, December 18):

> This is still day one. It's still the very beginning. We're not even in our awkward teenage years yet. Our mission is to be earth's most customer-centric company. We will raise the worldwide standard of what it means to be a customer-obsessed company.

Bezos' optimism aside, it's really too early to determine if Amazon will be one of the most notable success stories of the 21st century...or simply another dot.com company that flared brightly for a while before flaming out. The company will have to find a way to make a profit in the near future if it expects to keep attracting investors.

Jeffrey Bezos has done many things in correct fashion. He did the necessary research before he started his business, and he had the foresight to develop a business plan before he jumped into the market. He has definitely found a "niche," in the area of online book sales, and he seems to be expanding in areas that he understands and in areas that are somewhat related to his core business. He has hired good people, and he's retained the majority of these people despite a very volatile market.

Making a profit is the main goal at this point. This particular goal may have been acceptable when the high-tech market was booming and stocks with extremely high p/e ratios were the norm, but it is not acceptable in a more rational economy. Can Bezos turn his high-flying, money-losing Internet company into a more conventional, money-making enterprise? He seems to be on the right track. In January of 2002, Amazon fulfilled Jeffrey Bezos' prediction and posted a small profit. Although not significantly large, it was a respectable start. That the company made any profit at all during the economy at that particular time, would seem to bode well for the future.

References

Amazon.com. (2001). About Amazon.com: Company information. Retrieved November 17, 2001, from http://www.amazon.com.

Barker, J. (1989). *Discovering the future: The business of paradigms.* St. Paul, MN: ILI Press.

Brackett, V. (2001). *Jeff Bezos.* New York: 21st Century Publishing and Communications, Inc.

Brooker, K. (2000, December 18). Beautiful dreamer. *Fortune,* 142 (14), 234-244.

Saunders, R. (1999). *Business the Amazon.com way.* Dover, NH: Capstone Publishing Limited.

Spector, R. (2000). *Amazon.com get big fast.* New York: John Wiley & Sons, Inc.

The Company is not the stock. (2001, April 30). *Business Week,* 3730, 94-96.

Whiteley, L. (1999). *International directory of company histories* (Vol. 25). Detroit, MI: St. James Press.

Warren E. Buffett

Chairman and CEO
Berkshire Hathaway

*"You should invest in a business that even a fool can run,
because someday a fool will."* —Warren Buffett

Warren Buffett has been described as the world's greatest stock market investor. He is also known as the "Oracle of Omaha," the "Sage of Omaha" and the "Burger-Eating Billionaire." As an investor, Mr. Buffett is in a league of his own. He has been correctly reading the market for over five decades. In 1970, Buffett took over as CEO of Berkshire Hathaway Inc., a New England textile firm. Today, Buffett owns 38 percent of the company, which depending on the day-to-day fluctuations in the market is worth somewhere in the range of $36 billion dollars. The growth and success of Berkshire Hathaway was made possible without the use of hostile takeovers or leveraged buyouts (Price, 1998).

All this wealth seems to have had little impact on Warren's lifestyle. He still lives in the same house that he bought for $31,500 in 1957. He is not a connoisseur of caviar or champagne. Instead, he is big on burgers and Coca-Cola. Nor does he have a chauffeur; he drives his own car. He also does his own taxes. While many billionaires receive the ire of at least half the people that know of him, this is not the case with Warren Buffett.

He is highly regarded in many quarters for his knowledge, character, and wit. Warren Buffett is described as the "Will Rogers of Wall Street" and the "aw shucks" billionaire.

The Wit and Wisdom of Warren Buffett

Warren Buffett is quoted frequently within and outside the business world. His sage advice is usually peppered with a heavy dose of homespun Midwest humor. Here is a sample:

*"If past history was all there was to the game,
the richest people would be librarians."*

"Never ask the barber if you need a haircut."

*"As a group, lemmings have a rotten image,
but no individual lemming has ever received bad press."*

"Why not invest your assets in the companies you really like? As May West said, 'Too much of a good thing can be wonderful.'"

*"Wide diversification is only required when investors
do not understand what they are doing."*

*"With enough inside information and a million dollars,
you can go broke in a year."*

Early Life

Warren Buffett was born in Omaha, Nebraska, in 1930. His exceptional financial and entrepreneurial skills were fairly well developed before he left home. He was obviously influenced by his father Howard, who sold securities, stocks, and bonds for the Union Street Bank. Howard Buffett was also a Republican Congressman. Warren helped to mark the stock prices on the board at his father's brokerage firm when he was just 11. In that same year, he played the stock market for the first time. Warren bought three shares of Cities Service Preferred at $38 a share. To his surprise, the price immediately fell to $27. When the stock price bounced back to $40, he unloaded it only to see the stock price climb to $200 a share. He would rarely make this mistake again. Patience would become his strongest virtue (Kanter, 1999). He would later be quoted as saying:

"All there is to investing is picking good stocks at good
times and staying with them as long as they remain good companies."
—Business Legends

"What a company's stock sells for today, tomorrow, next week,
or next year doesn't matter. What counts is how the
company does over a five- or 10-year period."

His teenage business ventures included two paper routes, retrieving and reselling golf balls and managing pinball machines in local barbershops (Krass, 1999). When he was 14, he used $1,200 earned from his paper routes to buy 40 acres of Nebraska farmland. He then leased the land to a tenant farmer (Kanter, 1999). By the time he finished high school he had saved $5,000. This equates to over $42,000 today (Kennon, 2001).

At 17, Warren graduated from Woodrow Wilson High School in Washington, D.C. in 1947. Academically he was 16th in a class of 374 (Steele, 1999). His father urged him to go to the Wharton School of Finance at the University of Pennsylvania in Philadelphia. Warren appears to have not been happy there. He felt that he knew more about finance than his professors did. When his father failed to get re-elected to Congress in 1948, Warren used this as an opportunity to leave the University of Pennsylvania. He returned with his family to Omaha and then transferred to the University of Nebraska-Lincoln. Even though Warren worked full time while going to school, he was still able to get his bachelor's degree in just three years (Kennon, 2001).

During his last year at the University of Nebraska, Warren read *The Intelligent Investor* by Benjamin Graham. This book has been called the bible of the "value investors." Graham's book advises investors to ignore the fads of Wall Street and to instead search for stocks that trade far below their actual value (Kanter, 1999). Warren was greatly influenced by this book. In fact he called it "the greatest book on investing ever written" (Kennon, 2001).

After graduation, Warren was encouraged to apply to the Harvard Business School. Surprisingly, "the greatest investor of all time" was not accepted to Harvard because he was "too young" (Kanter, 1999). Many years later Warren described himself in his Harvard interview as "a scrawny nineteen-year-old who looked sixteen and had the poise of a twelve-year-old" (Steele, 1999). Warren then applied to Columbia University. This may have been where he really wanted to go all along since Columbia was the home of the famed investor Benjamin Graham whom Warren greatly admired. Buffett went on to study under Professor Graham and received a master's degree in economics from Columbia in 1951. Buffett freely acknowledges that Graham was the source of most of his ideas on investing (Cunningham). After graduation, Buffett would eventually work for his mentor at the Graham-Newman Corporation in New York City. He stayed with the investment firm until Graham retired in 1956. Buffet then moved back to Omaha to form a limited investment partnership.

Buffett Associates, Ltd. initially had seven partners who contributed a total of $105,000. Two of the partners were Warren's sister Doris and his aunt Alice. By the end of the year, the partnership had $300,000. Over the next five years, the partnership would show a profit of 251 percent. As a frame of reference, the Dow was up just 74% in the same time frame. By 1962, the partnership had over $7 million. Buffett's share was $1 million. In the ten years since its founding, the partnership assets had increased in value by more than 1,156%, to $44 million dollars. Again for contrast, the Dow was up by 122.9% in the same time frame. "In May 1969, he informed his partners that he was unable to find any bargains in the current market. Buffett spent the remainder of the year liquidating the portfolio, with the exception of two companies—Berkshire Hathaway and Diversified Retailing" (Kennon, 2001).

Berkshire Hathaway Inc.

The Berkshire Cotton Manufacturing Company was incorporated in 1889. Forty years later it combined with several other textile mills to become one of New England's largest textile mills. At its peak, Berkshire produced approximately 25 percent of the America's cotton products. In 1955, Berkshire merged with Hathaway Manufacturing. Unfortunately, things did not go well after the merger. Berkshire Hathaway's shareholder equity dropped by half in 10 years and losses from the operations reached $10 million. In 1962, Buffett began to purchase stock in this down-and-out textile mill located in New Bedford, Massachusetts. Why would Buffett be interested in a firm whose future seemed so bleak?

It wasn't just Berkshire Hathaway that was having trouble, the entire U.S. textile industry was getting creamed by foreign competition. Although it was trading for less than $8, Buffett concluded that it had a capital value of at least $16.50 per share. By 1965, the Buffett Partnership had controlling interest in the company. In 1970, Buffett named himself Chairman of the Board and Chief Executive Officer. During this time frame, Buffett began to re-deploy the firm's capital into a multitude of other "non-textile" businesses. In 1970, Berkshire Hathaway made $45,000 in its textile operations and $4.7 million in its non-textile operations (Kennon, 2001). Berkshire Hathaway's business activities were expanded to include the property and casualty insurance, candy, soft drinks, newspaper publishing, home furnishings, encyclopedias, home cleaning units, uniforms, jewelry, and footwear. The company would ultimately have substantial equity interests in such major corporations as American Express, Coca-Cola, GEICO, Walt Disney, Freddie Mac, Gillette, McDonald's, the *Washington Post,* and Wells Fargo (Cunningham, 2001). Buffett would eventually shut down all of Berkshire Hathaway's textile operations in 1985.

Hathaway would become Buffett's only vehicle for investing. He invested more than $15.4 million dollars in the company at the average cost of $32.45 per share. As a result he owned over 43% of the company's stock. By 1975, the company's book value had risen to $95 per share. In 1982 the stock value was $750 per share. During the 1990s it would go as high as $80,000 a share! (Kennon, 2001). The total value of the Berkshire-Hathaway holdings was in the neighborhood of $120 billion. In 1985, Warren Buffet would become a billionaire. In 1993, he would become the richest person in America (Steele, 1999).

Jeremy Siegel, a professor of finance at the Wharton School at the University of Pennsylvania, estimates that if a person had invested $1,000 with Buffett in the '60s, this would have turned into $61 million today. In contrast, had that $1,000 been invested in S&P 500 stocks, it would have grown to $100,000.

The annual meeting in Omaha for the 17,000 Berkshire Hathaway shareholders has been compared to "an Elvis concert or a religious revival." Buffett himself calls the meeting a "Woodstock for Capitalists." While most annual shareholder meetings are poorly attended and comatose, the annual Berkshire Hathaway meeting is a lively educational experience. Shareholders attend the annual meetings in increasing numbers each year. The CEO, Buffett, personally carries on a lengthy, enlightening, and straightforward dialogue with the shareholders.

People actually read the Berkshire Hathaway annual reports. The reason? While most annual reports are written to make the top management look good, Buffett writes his reports to actually provide valuable information. Shareholders will find a candid assessment of all the pluses and minuses of the company's operations. They are also laced with both wisdom and humor.

"If you want to be loved, it's clearly better to sell high-priced corn flakes than low-priced auto-insurance." —1988 Annual Report

"Fear is the foe of the faddist, but the friend of the fundamentalist."
—1994 Annual Report

Buffett's direct, educational and entertaining annual reports are available on the company's website at www.berkshirehathaway.com. Buffett's annual salary as the Chairman of the Board and the CEO of Berkshire Hathaway is $100,000 a year (Kanter, 1999).

Corporate Leadership

Berkshire Hathaway became a $50 billion enterprise because it invested in businesses that were both in good financial shape and had outstanding management. To Buffett, there are two very important criteria when he looks to acquire a company. First, does the company have a sustainable economic advantage? Buffett translates this esoteric economic concept into English: The company should be "a castle with a moat around it." Buffett said that when he was in business school he learned that "it doesn't help to be smarter than even your dumbest competitor. The trick is to have no competitors. That means having a product that truly differentiates itself" (Krass, 2001).

The second criterion to evaluate when acquiring a company is competent leadership. Companies "need honest, capable and hardworking leaders to retain their lead." Consequently a firm's management team is analyzed just as closely as the financial statements. In this regard, Buffett markedly departs from his mentor. Benjamin Graham was not really concerned about the corporate leadership so long as the finances were in order.

Buffett's "hands-off" leadership style gives each of Berkshire Hathaway's subsidiaries the "freedom to operate in whatever manner will best allow the company to exploit its strengths." Buffett says:

*"We subcontract all of the heavy lifting in this business
to the managers of our subsidiaries."*

Of Berkshire Hathaway's 45,000 employees, only twelve work at the company's main office in Omaha. Berkshire Hathaway's managers are given the following marching orders:

"Widen the moat. That keeps the castle valuable."

Buffett's leadership style works because he will only buy those companies that already have first-rate managers. He does not need to micromanage because the senior management already has an established track record of accomplishment. High on his list of desirable characteristics for a corporate leader are integrity, intelligence and energy. As Buffett says:

"If they don't have the first, the other two will kill you."

"The CEO who misleads others in public, may eventually mislead himself in private,"

"Anybody who trades away reputation for money is making a terrible mistake."

"It takes 20 years to build a reputation and five minutes to ruin it. If you think about that, you'll do things differently."

While Buffett views integrity as the most important trait in a corporate leader, intelligence is not far behind.

"There is the tendency for managers to behave like lemmings, imitating other managers rather than applying their abilities and knowledge on behalf of the business."

"A lemming-like willingness to follow the crowd endures, entailing the destruction of both leadership and independent thought."

"You are neither right nor wrong because the crowd disagrees with you. You are right because your data and reasoning are right."

"A public opinion poll is no substitute for thought."

"Risk comes from not knowing what you're doing."

"The best judgment we can make about managerial competence does not depend on what people say, but simply what the record shows."

Buffett equates intelligence in leadership with simplicity:

> *"There seems to be some perverse human characteristic*
> *that likes to make easy things difficult."*

> *"The business schools reward difficult complex behavior more than*
> *simple behavior, but simple behavior is more effective."*

> *"It is not necessary to do extraordinary things*
> *to get extraordinary results."*

In evaluating a company's senior leadership, Buffett asks three questions.

1. Is management rational?

2. Is management candid and forthright with shareholders?

3. Does management resist the institutional imperative?
                                        —(Buffett's Tenets)

This last question requires some elaboration. According to Buffett, the institutional imperative exists when:

1. An institution resists any change in its current direction;

2. Just as work expands to fill available time, corporate projects or acquisitions will materialize to soak up available funds;

3. Any business leader's craving, however foolish, will quickly be supported by detailed rate-of-return and strategic studies prepared by his troops; and

4. The behavior of peer companies, whether they are expanding, acquiring, setting executive compensation or whatever, will be mindlessly imitated (Bullock, 1998).

Warren Buffett feels that an excellent corporate leader should be well compensated. At Berkshire, Buffett rewards managers for their individual performance. This is based on their success at meeting specific performance goals keyed to their own area of responsibility. These measures are independent of Berkshire's overall corporate performance. A Warren Buffett aphorism captures this philosophy:

> *"The .350 hitter expects, and also deserves, a big payoff for his perfor-*
> *mance—even if he plays for a cellar-dwelling team. And a .150 hitter*
> *should get no reward—even if he plays for a pennant winner."*

On Organization Structure

Buffett observes that many companies are obsessed with organizational structure. He is not the least bit impressed with elaborate formulas or textbook rules on organizational behavior. Buffett believes that "mapping out an abstract chain of command on a particular business situation" is not the answer. "What matters is selecting people who are able, honest, and hard-working. Having first-rate people on the team is more important than designing hierarchies and clarifying who reports to whom about what and at what times." To Buffett, "the best solution is to take great care in identifying a CEO who will perform capably regardless of weak structural restraints" (Cunningham, 2001).

On Board of Directors

Outstanding CEOs do not need a lot of coaching from owners, although they can benefit from having a similarly outstanding board. Directors therefore must be chosen for their business savvy, their interest, and their owner-orientation. According to Buffett, one of the greatest problems among boards in corporate America is that members are selected for other reasons, such as adding diversity or prominence to a board. (Cunningham, 2001)

On Costs

> Whenever I read about some company undertaking a cost-cutting program, I know it's not a company that really knows what costs are all about. Spurts don't work in this area. The really good manager does not wake up in the morning and say, "This is the day I'm going to cut costs," any more than he wakes up and decides to practice breathing. (Wisdom)

Buffett found that managers of high-cost operations continually add to overhead, whereas managers of low-cost operations are always finding ways to cut expenses. Berkshire Hathaway is in the latter category. It is a low-cost operation with after-tax overhead corporate expense of less than 1 percent of operating earnings (Bullock, 1998).

Coca-Cola

Buffett seeks out businesses that he would feel good about owning. He is less concerned with charts or numbers. His focus is on the business that a company is in and their management (Krass, 2001).

Steps to selecting companies:

1. We start by only looking at companies we understand.

2. We observe whether or not the management is telling us the truth in the Annual Report and other publications. We avoid companies with annual reports full of PR gobbledygook. We want to be able to read the report and know the company better at the end.

Coca Cola was a company that met both of his criteria. It had a strong brand image with a positive track record spanning decades. Warren understood the product. In fact, he immensely enjoyed drinking Coke with his meals.

Buffett found the Coca Cola's Annual Report to be extremely informative as well. He bought a big chunk of Coca Cola's stock based on just their reports alone. He had not had any discussions with the Coca Cola management. He liked this company's candid straightforward style of communication (Price, 1998).

Solomon Brothers

In 1991, Buffett was called upon to lead a major company besides his own, albeit for a short time. Buffett was on the Board of Directors of Solomon Brothers. The company was not doing well at the time. There was a lot of red ink flowing. This may help to explain why the company got into trouble with both the Treasury Department and the SEC. An employee of Solomon, Paul Mozer, was using the cover of two institutional clients, Mercury and Quantum Funds, as a way to illegally purchase Treasury bonds. No firm was allowed to have more than 35 percent of the total. By using Mercury and Quantum as a vehicle to buy the bonds, Solomon Brother's was able to obtain 57 percent of the total.

When the Treasury Department came to Mercury asking questions, an executive at Mercury called Mr. Mozer asking him to explain what was going on. Mozer said that it was a mistake. Mozer then notified the upper management at Solomon about the incident. These executives decided to keep this mistake under wraps even though their legal counsel recommended that they come clean with the Feds. Nothing would have come of this incident, except that Mr. Mozer did it again. This time he obtained not 57 percent of the total but 87 percent. Alarms went off as other firms claimed that Solomon Brothers was trying to corner the market on T-Bills. The SEC was called in to investigate. They found, not two, but six instances of bidding violations. As a result, heads rolled. All of the senior Solomon executives involved in the cover-up were summarily fired.

The fate of Solomon Brothers became very much in doubt. They had no senior management and the Federal Government was trying to decide how big a hammer they were going to use on Solomon Brothers. It was at this point that Warren Buffett was named CEO of Solomon Brothers. Buffett's business partner at Berkshire, Charles Munger, was totally opposed to the idea. "The risk to his professional life was enormous; indeed, his entire reputation hung on the line. Howie warned his father that 'everyone who ever wanted to take a shot at you is going to do it'" (Kennon, 2001).

Shortly after he took over the company, the Treasury Department made it known that it intended to ban Solomon Brothers from participating in Federal auctions. This action would have effectively shut down Solomon Brothers' $150 billion operation. Buffett appealed to the Federal Reserve and Alan Greenspan to reconsider. In the end, Solomon Brothers had its trading privileges reinstated. Buffett had no intention of staying on as the CEO. He would lead the company only long enough to get it through this traumatic period.

"As in his operating companies, Buffett wanted the leader identified. Although he was currently the acting CEO, it was important for him to know who would eventually lead the firm after his corporate CPR was done. He individually pulled the upper managers into a room and asked them who they thought should run the company" (Kennon, 2001).

Up Close and Personal

Although Warren Buffett has had extensive links to the East Coast (Washington DC, Philadelphia, and New York City), he prefers to live in Omaha. A colleague gave this as the reason: "Warren's kept his perspective clear by living in Omaha, away from it all, and looking at what's important rather than what's urgent or fashionable" (Krass, 2001). He continues to live in a modest gray stucco house that he calls Buffett's Folly. While Warren comes across as a natural conversationalist, he had an intense fear of public speaking. To overcome this fear, he took a Dale

Carnegie course on public speaking. After he had gained confidence in speaking, he started teaching Investment Principles at the University of Nebraska. Most of his students were over twice his age. He was just 21 at the time (Kennon, 2001).

Warren's relationship with his wife Susan is rather unconventional. They were married in 1952 and had three children: Susie, Howard, and Peter. However, when Susan was 45, she decided that she needed to "find herself." As a part-time cabaret singer, humanitarian, and passionate abortion-rights activist, Susan must have found life in Omaha "confining." She left Warren in 1977 and moved into an apartment in San Francisco. A year later, Susan introduced Warren to Astrid Menks, a Latvian-born waitress who worked at the French Cafe in Omaha. Within the year, Astrid moved in with Warren. She has been his "companion" ever since. Warren and his wife Susan have remained close over the years. Susan accompanies Warren on almost all of his public appearances. She also serves on Berkshire's board and is one of the firm's largest shareholders. Susan and Astrid have remained friends as well. In fact, the three send presents to relatives from "Warren, Susie and Astrid" (Kanter, 1999).

Even though his father had been a Republican Congressman, Warren appears to be a liberal Democrat. "In the late 1960s, he became involved in abortion rights issues and worked to integrate Omaha's segregated country clubs" (Kanter, 1999).

Warren Buffett is often is criticized for being a tightwad (*Maybe that helps to explain why he is a billionaire!*). His Buffett Foundation was established in the mid-1960s as a vehicle to distribute his wealth. Each year, the Foundation disburses between $11 million and $12 million. Considering that Buffett is worth billions, this is not exactly "tithing." Most of this goes to family-planning clinics. Although he has three children, his wife Susan is his sole heir. Buffett has said that he intends to leave 99 percent of his money to the Buffett Foundation. This will make it the largest endowment in the country (Kanter, 1999).

His frugal reputation extends to his children as well. On one occasion Warren's daughter Susie needed $20 to get her car out of the airport garage. He helped her but then "he made her write him a check" (Kanter, 1999). For Warren everything is strictly business. When his son Howard said that he wanted to purchase a farm, Buffett was willing to help. However, it was not exactly a father-son arrangement. Warren presented his son with some very exacting business terms. Warren would buy the farm and rent it back to his son. Howie would also be required to pay a percentage of the farm income back to his father as well as pay the taxes. Howie agreed to his father's terms. Warren, however, did not show much interest in his son's endeavor. He visited the farm only twice in six years (Kanter, 1999).

For all Warren Buffet's billions, he is not into expensive food, clothes or cars. He enjoys burgers and Coca-Cola (a company that he has invested in since 1988). His suits (often crumpled) are always off-the-shelf and he keeps his cars for five years. However, Warren does have one indulgence: Corporate Aircraft and luxury air travel. In 1986, Buffett bought a used Falcon aircraft for $850,000. Commercial travel was becoming less practical as he became a celebrity. His infatuation for this luxury jet influenced his decision to acquire the Executive Jet Company (Kennon, 2001). He calls his current jet, a Gulfstream IV-SP, "The Indefensible" (Kanter, 1999).

Two other little known facts about Warren Buffett: 1. He plays the ukulele, and 2. He plays bridge with his good friend, Bill Gates (Symanovich, 2001).

Conclusion—Just Remember "Lemmings" and "Moats"

During the 1990s, Warren Buffett was accused (*by non-billionaires*) of being "out of touch" with the market. When he chose to sit out the dot.com and technology stock stampede, a number of newspapers ran stories about the demise of "The Oracle of Omaha." However, Warren Buffett's actions during this buying frenzy were completely in keeping with his decades old and immensely successful investment strategy. He had always talked about going the opposite direction of the "lemmings" and seeking out companies that were "surrounded by a moat." If a company's product or service is not sufficiently differentiated from its competitors, then it has little or no "moat" to protect it. When it came to the dot.coms and the technology stocks, the "lemmings" were definitely stampeding, which was not a good sign. With technology changing so quickly, few firms were able to maintain a dominant position. The latest and greatest cell phones were obsolete in six months. In other words, the technology firms did not have any "moat" to speak of. Buffett was simply following his own advice:

Never invest in a business you cannot understand.
(Buffett is a self-described "technophobe")

*Only buy companies with strong histories of profitability
and with a dominant business franchise.*
(The dot.com and technology companies had no history and no "moat")

Look for companies with high profit margins
(These companies for the most part did not ever show a profit)

*Be fearful when others are greedy and greedy
only when others are fearful.*
(This is the self-explanatory "lemming" rule)

Buffett's patience during the dot.com hysteria certainly paid off. He was well positioned for what he saw as an inevitable crash. Even though Buffett's investment philosophy has not changed in 55 years, he is once again being championed as "The Oracle of Omaha."

Buffett's Final Goal:

*What I want people to say when they pass by my casket is,
"Boy, was he old!"*

References

Buffett's Tenets. (n.d.) *Commonly referred to sayings of Warren Buffett.* Retrieved August 1, 2002, from http://www.anglefire.com/co/ simplewealth/buffettips.html

Bullock, I. (1998). *Warren Buffett's investment checklist.* Retrieved August 1, 2002, from http://www.refresher.com/!buffett2.html

Cunningham, L. A. (2001). *The essays of Warren Buffett: Lessons for corporate America.* Retrieved August 1, 2002, from http://www.cardozo.yu.edu/heyman/wbintro.html

Kanter, L. (1999, August 31). *People: Warren Buffett.* Retrieved August 1, 2002, from http://www.salon.com/people/bc/1999/08/31/buffett/ index1.html

Kennon, J. (2001). *Warren Buffett: A short biography.* Retrieved August 1, 2002, from http://beginnersinvest.about.com/library/titans/ nwarrenbio.htm

Krass, P. (Ed.). (1999). *The book of investing wisdom: Classic writings by great stock pickers and legends of Wall Street.* Retrieved August 1, 2002, from http://www.tradinglibrary.it/abstract/ 0471294543krassextract.txt

Price, J. (1998). *Berkshire Hathaway and the Buffetteers: The return of the Buffetteers.* Retrieved August 1, 2002, from http:// www.sherlockinvesting.com/articles/buffetteers.htm

Steele, J. (1999) *Warren Buffett: Master of the market.* New York: Avon.

Symanovich, S. (2001, April 6). *Music maker jams with Warren Buffett.* Retrieved August 1, 2002, from http://www.bizjournals.com/ sanfrancisco/stories/2001/04/09/editorial1.html

Wisdom from business legends. (n.d.). Retrieved August 1, 2002, from http://www.angelfire.com/nv/InspirationUniv/quotes/11.html

Kenneth I. Chenault

President and Chief Operating Officer
American Express

The Early Years

Kenneth Irvine Chenault was born June 2, 1951, in Mineola, New York. His parents' success in the dentistry profession had a lasting impression on Ken, and his admiration for his parents has had a profound effect on his life. Ken particularly revered his father, Dr. Hortenius Chenault, who died in 1990. Said the younger Chenault, "My father's basic view was that you really needed to concentrate on the things you can control…and what you can control is your own performance" (Bianco, 1998). Although somewhat of an academic "late bloomer," Ken Chenault was extraordinarily intelligent. He was an avid reader and enjoyed studying history.

During his high school years, Ken made a valiant attempt to apply his skills in the classroom. By the time he was a senior, he had achieved honor role status and was elected as president of his class. Additionally, he excelled in athletics. He was selected as the team captain of the school's basketball, soccer, and track teams (Current Biography Yearbook, 1998). These early leadership roles were instrumental in his later success as a leader in the business world.

*"As a kid, I knew I wanted to be a leader in something.
I just didn't know what."* —Kenneth Chenault

Chenault started his college career at Springfield College with the assistance of an athletic scholarship. After only one year at Springfield, he decided to transfer to Bowdoin College. At the time of his transfer, the student body consisted of approximately 950 students...and only 24 of these were of African American descent. Chenault worked hard and won the respect of both classmates and faculty for his ability to debate racial issues. In 1973, he graduated with a B.A. degree, magna cum laude, with honors in history (Current Biography Yearbook, 1998).

After graduation, Chenault entered Harvard University Law School. He received his J.D. degree in 1976. While attending Harvard, he met Kathryn Cassell. He and Kathryn dated and eventually married on August 20, 1977. They currently reside in New York and have two sons, Kenneth Jr. and Kevin.

Chenault's first employment after law school was as an associate at the New York City law firm of Rogers & Wells. After two years, he was recruited by Bain & Co., a business consulting firm in Boston. He stayed there about two years and was then hired as director of strategic planning for American Express.

Moving up the Corporate Ladder

After two years in strategic planning at American Express, Chenault was promoted to Vice President in charge of Merchandise Services. In this capacity, he was credited with upscaling the merchandise line by offering name-brand watches, leather luggage, and several other high-quality products. He was also able to cut order time by half, using improved technology and a new management structure. His efforts did not go unnoticed, and he was promoted to Senior Vice President of Merchandise Services.

By 1986, Chenault was promoted to Executive Vice President and General Manager of American Express's Platinum and Gold Cards Division. He served in this capacity until 1989, when he received an important promotion to President of the Consumer Card and Financial Services Group.

At the time Chenault took over as President of this group, American Express was well known in the industry for its green, gold, and platinum cards. The company was unique in that it still required members to pay the total balance due on their credit cards at the end of each month…even though Visa and MasterCard were offering (indeed, encouraging) their customers to take several months to pay.

In 1987, a year before Chenault took over as President of the group, American Express introduced the Optima card. This card belatedly offered revolving credit…in an attempt to compete directly with Visa and MasterCard. Unfortunately, American Express offered the Optima card only to established green, gold, and platinum cardholders.

The rationale behind this decision was that existing American Express cardholders would be less likely to default on paying bills. In reality, however, almost the exact opposite occurred. Optima card users incurred about twice as much bad debt as had been anticipated.

In analyzing this phenomenon after the fact, American Express determined that their customers (all of whom also carried American Express cards) would use the American Express card for necessary and non-discretionary purchases that they intended to pay off at the end of the month. This left the Optima Card for unnecessary and discretional purchases that they wanted to delay payment on…or purchases that they weren't sure when they would ever be able to pay in full. This resulted in higher-than-average losses and unpaid balances for the Optima card and a big decline in profits for American Express (Current Biography Yearbook, 1998).

Fortunately for Chenault, Optima had been formed as a separate group within Travel Related Services (TRS). This particular group was separate from the consumer Card and Financial Services Group, so Chenault was not directly to blame for the Optima fiasco. Despite this, however, he felt compelled to make recommendations for some specific changes within the organization.

Another big obstacle that Chenault had to contend with was a threatened boycott of restaurant owners in 1991. The owners were upset that the fee imposed on them by American Express was higher than the fees charged by Visa or MasterCard. Mr. Chenault traveled to Boston to minimize the effects of what journalists had dubbed the "Boston Fee Party," and his negotiation skills and impeccable composure preserved the company's relationship with the restaurateurs. After substantial negotiation, Chenault agreed to lower certain fees…including the fees on charges that were submitted electronically. This decision resulted in both parties being satisfied, and was a true win-win situation. The restaurateurs felt that they had gained what they were after, and American Express was able to remain competitive in the industry (Current Biography Yearbook, 1998).

In his ongoing efforts to tailor the American Express card to customers' needs, Chenault introduced a "frequent flier" program where members could earn free flights by simply using the American Express card. Since the two largest airlines already had partnered with competitive credit card companies, American Express took the unique step of partnering itself with seven carriers including big names such as Delta, Northwest, and Continental.

In hindsight, an airline partnership should have been consummated back in the mid-1980s when American Airlines extended an invitation to American Express to become the first credit card company to award their customers frequent flier mileage. In fact, the *New York Times* (July 30, 1995) called American Express's refusal "the worst business decision ever." Nonetheless, Chenault was credited with moving the company in the right direction.

When Harvey Golub became CEO of American Express, he promoted Chenault to President of the U.S. operations of Travel Related Services (TRS). This was an exceptionally important leadership position within the company. Chenault's responsibilities now included the Consumer Card and Financial Services Group, the Travel Services Group, consumer lending activities, and the Optima card division.

In 1994, Golub and Chenault agreed that the company should shift its focus to cards offering revolving credit. Not surprisingly, the decision was met with skepticism based on the earlier problems associated with Optima. Chenault met all of this negativity with enthusiasm and with a strong conviction that this new program would be successful.

His spirit and determination carries to this day and, since the inception of this new card, which was called the Optima True Grace card, the company has introduced several different new cards. These new cards are tailored to meet the specific needs and wants of specific target audiences. For example, American Express has introduced cards targeted to college students, senior citizens, travelers, golfers, etc.

In 1995, in the midst of implementing the new American Express strategy, Mr. Chenault was once again promoted...this time to Vice Chairman of American Express. At the same time, he was given the additional responsibility of overseeing TRS International, one of the largest segments of the organization.

President and Chief Operating Officer

After gaining two years of experience as Vice Chairman, Mr. Chenault's efforts earned him yet another promotion…to President and Chief Operating Officer. Along with this promotion, came the announcement that Ken Chenault was the heir-apparent to American Express Chairman Harvey Golub. Mr. Chenault would soon become one of the first African Americans to earn the title of CEO of a Fortune 500 company.

> *"There have been a number of people before and after me who clearly possess the capabilities to run a large firm. That's why it's so important to look at me not as an exception but rather as someone who was given the opportunity to succeed."*
> —Kenneth Chenault

News of Chenault's promotion to President and COO…and news that he had been promised the CEO position…spread like wildfire. Both inside and outside the company, this news was greeted with approval and delight. As one American Express Division President noted:

> You would go in the elevators and hear, 'Isn't it exciting about Ken? Can you believe that Ken got promoted? Isn't it fantastic?' 'Oh, I feel much better about the company now that Ken is President.' People wrote him notes; he was flooded with e-mail; there were flowers and calls from corporate and political leaders (as cited in Pierce, 1997).

Breaking the Glass Ceiling

Chenault's heir-apparent designation as CEO was considered deserving and long overdue. It was also seen as an extremely positive sign for other hopeful African American executives. Mr. Chenault's appointment was viewed in the minority community as confirmation that, when given a chance, African Americans are not only willing, but eager and able to successfully lead Fortune 500 companies.

Diversity experts, noting an overall increase in minority participation at the upper echelons of Corporate America, viewed Chenault's up-and-coming CEO status as a very important signal that America was on the way to achieving a bias-free workplace. Indeed, many statements were made that seemed to make Chenault into a second Martin Luther King…a leader who could single-handedly break down barriers that had stood for years. One such message included the following:

When that obstacle is broken and you have an African American who is the CEO of a Fortune 500 company, the message to corporate America will be that we can do an outstanding job when these selections are made. To the black community, this will ignite hope and desire. It's never been that we can't handle these positions but rather have been denied access. And when that day comes, it will be a great day. (Harvey, as cited in Smith, 1997)

A humble and reserved Chenault tried to downplay his CEO in-waiting status, but many of America's minorities seem determined to make him into a folk hero, a role model and a precursor of many good things to come. The statement below substantiates this claim:

His appointment signals what the possibilities are for African Americans. There always has to be a first, then a second and third. But breaking that barrier and being first is always the most difficult. His appointment can only help pave the way for others. (Hinds, as cited in Smith, 1997)

Ann Fudge, President of Maxwell House Coffee Co. and one of the first black women to reach the upper echelon of corporate America, echoes Mr. Hinds' sentiments:

All of this corporate reengineering has forced people to look at their performers with a lot more scrutiny. That gives talented people...regardless of their race or gender...an opportunity to make an impression, the kind that counts when it's time to see who moves up. We're in this race like everybody else, and everybody's not going to win. But when the first breakthrough is made, it'll be terrific for a lot of reasons, and largely because I'll know what they had to go through to get there. (Smith, 1997)

The "People-Person" Chenault

Arguably, one of Ken Chenault's greatest skills is his "soft" or "people" skills. He is a warm and caring individual, and he has the keen knack of being able to motivate his troops while being able to criticize without actually humiliating. He has the ability to get people to do what they thought they could never achieve. He inspires through respect, not fear. According to one of his colleagues:

He's the most human of all chief executives I've worked with. He has extraordinary listening skills; he actively wants to hear your opinions. A senior executive can spend 15 minutes with

Ken and be motivated for the next month without any more contact. Ken engenders a kind of loyalty that money can't buy.

He can also make the painful bearable. When American Express had to take $1.4 billion out of the company's expenses, which included letting go 12,000 people from 1991-1994, Ken was the point person. He would talk to the troops, share their pain, but convince them the cuts were necessary and unavoidable. (Pierce, 1997)

In his typical humble fashion, Ken describes his take on leadership and being the leader of an organization. As an avid athlete, he shares his thoughts with a sports analogy.

You analyze the opposing team, the plays, the moves, what are the rules of the game, the weaknesses that can be exploited and the strengths that need to be dealt with. The coach has to understand the capabilities of the different members of the team, to inspire people, to instill hope. The coach is accountable for the performance of the team. (Pierce, 1997)

Many top executives acknowledge the concept of teamwork but, when successful, few are willing to share credit with others involved in the process. They eagerly take credit for all successes, yet just as eagerly shift blame to underlings when failure results. Chenault is the exception to this philosophy. He considers himself the team leader...but not its boss. He believes an integral part of success is to share credit when credit is due. He seeks out his employees' input. In fact, Chenault hosts monthly "brown-bag" lunches with employees of all levels throughout the organization. He proudly explains, "I've gotten some of my best ideas this way" (Chenault, as cited in Shook, 1997).

An Earlier Start than Expected

To everyone's surprise, the future arrived early for Ken Chenault. On April 26, 2000, Mr. Golub announced he would cede the CEO title to Chenault in 2001, earlier than his originally stated date. Additionally, Chenault would assume the role as Chairman one year later, in 2002.

Mr. Golub had earlier indicated that he intended to retire at age 65. He clarified his statement when he noted that the timing had been arbitrary. He had since decided to stop working for the company earlier to pursue other interests...perhaps even a law degree (Beckett, 1999).

Chenault will not be the first African American to reach the top position at a Fortune 500 company. However, no other black individual has controlled a financial services organization that operates on such a global basis.

One consultant suggested that Chenault is a confident man who cares about bringing results to company shareholders.

> If a man at that level—black, white, or green—doesn't have a certain amount of ego or fire, then he can't do the job. You have to be pleasant to be around, but decisive and clinical about your decisions while remaining humane, and he has all those qualities. (as cited in Whigham-Desir, 1999)

He got the 'fire' from his father, whom, he says, was very achievement-oriented, and impressed upon him the need to maintain his personal and professional obligations and commitments. His mother, Anne, taught him how to listen and be open while maintaining balance in his life (Whigham-Desir, 1999).

Many of Chenault's current and former colleagues suggest that Chenault's personality is unique. None recall him losing his temper or even raising his voice. He invariably will take time to "small talk" with secretaries when he phones their superiors. Additionally, he has given his time to mentor numerous up-and-coming promising American Express managers. Although a well thought-out, methodical decision maker, he is not only open to input from subordinates, but encourages them to speak their mind (Bianco, 1998).

Some "Big Shoes to Fill"

When Chenault actually took over at the helm on January 1, 2001, he realized that being the leader of a Fortune 500 company would not be easy. Living up to the legend of Harvey Golub would be difficult as well. Chenault would have to deal with the increasing cutthroat competition of the credit card industry. Additionally, he was charged with continuing company growth during an economic time when consumer spending was on a downslide. Chenault had to be cognizant of the debilitating effects of the slowing economy on the American Express from years ago when the economy dwindled. Said one analyst from J.P. Morgan, "Ken Chenault's biggest challenge is something he has absolutely no control over—the economy" (as cited in Schwartz, 2001).

"No one is hoping the economy goes south. But if it does, we will use this environment to inflict some pain on specific competitors as well as gain market share." —Ken Chenault

If anyone can handle the pressure, Chenault is the person. His leadership has its own kind of charisma…a peculiar type of warmth that allows people to feel at ease and be a part of his team.

Throughout his 20-plus years at American Express, Chenault has established a reputation as both a marketer and a revenue builder. He is considered by his colleagues and American Express employees as even-tempered and fair, known for implementing cost-cutting measures (even closing entire divisions) while still managing to keep employee loyalty and respect. His image is that of modesty, which is a different image than that of his predecessor. Despite these differences, the two leaders of the organization worked exceptionally well together. In the early 1990s, both company revenue and share value plummeted. However, through the efforts of Chenault and Golub, the company made a drastic turnaround.

One major area where Chenault's experience and reputation will be tested is in the company's use of the Internet. In early 1999, investors were somewhat baffled by where American Express's Internet website was heading. Although the company had developed a website, they appeared to flounder with regard to where the site was headed and what it was intended to accomplish.

In the interim, both Visa and MasterCard appeared to leapfrog over American Express with regard to Internet sites. Prior to handing over the CEO leadership role, Golub conceded that the company's biggest challenge was to develop an Internet strategy "that will have some long lasting effect" (D'apos-Ambrosio, 2001). Chenault made the Internet his top priority and by mid-1999, the company's Internet strategy began to evolve. New products with online components became available, American Express opened a "virtual" bank, and an online discount brokerage was offered. Finally, a business-to-business Web marketplace was introduced.

Measuring Chenault's Performance

Chenault has also pushed to expand the company's traditional green credit card with the introduction of new credit cards. His most significant card introduction was Blue. This was a Web-oriented credit card aimed at the younger marketplace, and was the first card that contained a microchip to provide for extra security for online purchases.

The Blue card has two important benefits for American Express:

- It increases brand awareness because it allows American Express to build on one of its hallmarks...doing whatever necessary to please and protect cardholders.

- It gave American Express some credibility and believability with younger people who thought of the traditional green card as "stodgy"...something used by their parents in an earlier era (D'apos-Ambrosio, 2001).

Following the introduction of Blue, Private Payments hit the market. This provided shoppers with the security of typing their legitimate credit card numbers onto the screen, while a different (fictitious) number went into cyberspace. The cyberspace number would automatically change with every consumer purchase.

Since security issues are one of consumers biggest concerns regarding online purchasing, both Blue and Private Payments are seen by the experts as sure victories for American Express.

Mr. Chenault has also become adept at combining different sectors of the company such as the travel, credit card, and Internet units in an effort to enhance various promotions. For instance, he has made it possible for customers to book travel and make purchases while navigating the same area on American Express's website. Chenault's Internet directives to his people are threefold:

- Make the American Express Website "a superior experience"

- Make customer service as strong online as it is in the physical world

- Cut organizational costs

Another major change that Chenault has made is a new corporate policy and emphasis with regard to joint ventures. He has made it clear that, under his leadership, joint ventures will be an integral part of the company's success.

One of the most important lessons we've learned is that we can't—and shouldn't—do everything on our own. It does not make economic sense to build new divisions or buy other companies in order to be able to meet all of your customers' needs. (D'apos-Ambrosio, 2001)

The Devastating 9/11 Blow

Without a doubt, Mr. Chenault's greatest challenge since becoming CEO of American Express was the way in which he demonstrated leadership in dealing with the aftermath of the terrorist attack of September 11, 2001. Millions of television viewers got their first glimpse of Ken Chenault on October 3, 2001, when he was seated next to George W. Bush, who was in the city to provide reassurance and support to the world.

The company's world headquarters building was uninhabitable after the attack and Chenault, along with the other 3,200 American Express employees who were housed in the headquarters building, had to find a new work area. Chenault took the lead in finding new working quarters and also managed to portray a calm and positive image in the face of all the confusion and hysteria that marked the aftermath of the attack. As one writer said of Mr. Chenault, "The role of the leader is to define reality and give hope. And this certainly was the year where it was important to constantly do both" (Roberts, 2002).

Even prior to September's tragedy, the picture at American Express wasn't very pretty because the unpredictable stock market had taken its toll on the company's money management business. After the terrorist attacks, the company's core travel services and charge card businesses were hurt substantially by the weakening economy (Roberts, 2002).

When combining all of the different problems facing American Express today, it may seem that Mr. Chenault has what many consider an insurmountable task ahead of him. Yet, if ever there is a leader to successfully accomplish this task, Chenault might well be the person. He has an uncanny ability to take an unbiased view of his company, and that will inevitably be critical in rebuilding the American Express organization.

Chenault, who has rightfully been praised for his calm demeanor despite adversity, says that what concerns him most at this time is the trauma wreaked on his employees. Yet he also points out their willingness to come together as one when needed:

> Our greatest loss from the September 11 terrorist attacks was the loss of life. We are supporting the families in whatever way we can, particularly the 11 children these employees have left behind.
>
> In addition, there is the emotional trauma faced by all of our employees in the building that day. They had to be evacuated...and were witnesses to the horrific events across the street.

We're focused on serving our customers and clients. Immediately after the attacks, we saw employees make decisions and take action—without being told, without being asked. They helped thousands of stranded consumers and corporate travelers get home by airplane, train, bus and rental car. They extended service hours. They proactively called customers to review and revise financial plans. They provided emergency cash when needed. Their goal was to ensure that our clients were served, and they succeeded. This commitment to customer service is embedded in our corporate culture. (Norment, 2002)

The difficulties imposed by the terrorist attack, combined with the difficulties already facing American Express, might daunt a lot of leaders. But Chenault is not only a proud man...he is also a fighter, and a man who has unique outlook on the responsibilities of a leader in today's complex world. In his own words:

In today's new environment, leaders need to help people cope, give them hope and confidence—not just for the sake of the company, but for the broader purpose of supporting and renewing our country and way of life. I have also learned that it is during such tough times that we learn if our values, beliefs, and relationships are enduring. As leaders, we must recognize that there is no manual describing how to proceed. Instead, we must make our values our anchor in order to succeed. (Norment, 2002)

The Future of American Express?

Despite the obstacles Mr. Chenault has experienced, he is quite optimistic about the future of both his company and American business in general.

There is no doubt that American Express faces challenges, but because of the strength and quality of our people, I have confidence that American Express will emerge from this tragedy even better and stronger. As a nation, we mourn the loss of family, friends, and people we never even knew. But we are more united than ever. The spirit of Americans both inside and outside of New York has risen to a whole new level. As a result, I firmly believe that we will rebuild New York City, we will revitalize our economy, and our way of life will survive and prosper. (Norment, 2002)

References

Beckett, P. (1999, April 27). American Express CEO announces 2001 retirement and successor. *Wall Street Journal* [eastern edition], p. A.4. Retrieved April 9, 2002, from ProQuest Direct database on the World Wide Web: http://proquest.umi.com.

Bianco, A. (1998, December 21). The rise of a star. *Business Week*, 3609, 60. Retrieved April 10, 2002, from ProQuest Direct database on the World Wide Web: http://proquest.umi.com.

Current biography yearbook. (1998). New York: The H.W. Wilson Company.

D'apos-Ambrosio, M. (2001, January-February). It's time to put the 'E' in Amex: American Express CEO Kenneth Chenault must craft the company's Internet vision while also upping its stake in the payments business. *Future Banker* 5, 1. Retrieved April 9, 2002, from Infotrac Direct database on the World Wide Web: http://web5.infotrac.galegroup.com.

No. 1: Ken Chenault, CEO, American Express: Overhauled the Executive Suite. Then he went to work. *Future Banker*, 5, 4. Retrieved April 17, 2002, from Infotrac Direct database on the World Wide Web: http://web5.infotrac.galegroup.com.

Norment, L. (2002, February). 3 at the top: Major executives tell how they are dealing with the crisis. *Ebony*, 57, 4. Retrieved April 10, 2002, from ProQuest Direct database on the World Wide Web http://proquest.umi.com.

Pierce, P. (1997, July). Blazing new paths in corporate America. *Ebony*, 52, 9. Retrieved April 12, 2002, from ProQuest Direct database on the World Wide Web: http://proquest.umi.com.

Roberts, J. (2002, January 28). The race to the top. *Newsweek,* 139, 4. Retrieved April 10, 2002, from ProQuest Direct database on the World Wide Web: http://proquest.umi.com.

Schwartz, N. (2001, January 22). What's in the cards for Amex? *Fortune*, 58-70. Retrieved April 10, 2002, from ProQuest Direct database on the World Wide Web: http://proquest.umi.com .

Shook, C. (1997, December 1). Leader, not boss. *Forbes*, 52-54. Retrieved April 10, 2002, from ProQuest Direct database on the World Wide Web: http://proquest.umi.com.

Smith, E. (1997, May). Someone's knocking at the door: Kenneth Chenault's appointment as President and COO of American Express threatens to shatter one of the final barriers to corporate America's top spot. *Black Enterprise*, 27, 10. Retrieved April 17, 2002, from Infotrac Direct database on the World Wide Web: http://web5.infotrac.galegroup.com.

Whigham-Desir, M. (1999, September). Leadership has its rewards. *Black Enterprise,* 30, 2. Retrieved April 9, 2002, from Infotrac Direct database on the World Wide Web: http://web5.infotrac.galegroup.com.

Michael Dell

Chairman and Chief Executive Officer
Dell Computer Corporation

"I didn't know, at age eighteen, how big the opportunity would become, but I knew that was what I wanted to do." —Michael Dell

Michael Dell is a highly successful CEO in one of the most cutthroat of all industries: the computer business. He holds two very unique distinctions that would appear to be incompatible. Mr. Dell is the youngest CEO of all the major computer companies and he has held this position since 1984. That's a longer tenure than anyone else in the industry. In 1992, at the age of 27, he was the youngest CEO to head a Fortune 500 company. In the time that he has been the Chairman and Chief Executive Officer of the Dell Computer Corporation, Compaq has had two CEOs, Hewlett-Packard has had three, and Apple has had four.

He is clearly one of the wealthiest men in America. By owning 14 percent of the company, Dell is worth over $20 billion (Cringely, 2001). To put this in perspective, Michael Dell has a greater net worth than did Bill Gates at the same age (Verespej, 1998). The adjectives most frequently used to describe the leadership traits of this self-made billionaire from Houston are "visionary" "entrepreneurial" and "hands-on."

The Early Years

> *"I became very interested in computers when I was young, and my
> interest soon evolved from a hobby into a business opportunity. I
> wanted to learn as much as I could about PCs, so I would take them
> apart and then rebuild them with enhanced components."*
> —Michael Dell

Michael Dell started his mega billion-dollar computer business in 1984
while he was a student at the University of Texas. He was just 18 at the
time with only $1,000 in his pocket (www.dell.com). He realized that the
$3,000 computers that were being sold in the local retail stores only had
about $700 worth of parts in them (Cringely, 2001). With this knowledge,
he began to assemble and sell computers out of his dorm room to his
fellow students at prices far below the retail price. Dell also noticed "that
the people who were operating computer stores didn't know much about
PCs and couldn't offer much in the way of support" (Q&A). So besides
beating the retail price, Dell also provided a superior product and quality
service. His operation became so lucrative that he moved his business out
of his dorm room and into a condominium off campus. Prior to this move,
his monthly sales were between $50,000 and $80,000. At the end of his
freshman year in 1984, he opted to drop out of college so that he could
pursue his business full time. The Dell name for the company came later.
From 1984 to 1989 the company was called "PC's Limited" (Cringely,
2001).

Dell's unorthodox vision was to sell custom-built computer systems
directly to end-users and bypass the middleman. It was Dell's opinion
that the middleman and the extensive retail infrastructure added very little
to the value of the product. At the time, many were skeptical that such a
direct-sell business, most often associated with clothing, could ever work
for computers. Those skeptics were wrong (McWilliams, 1997). In just
17 years, his direct-sell vision has grown from $6 million in annual sales
into a Fortune 500 company with over $32 billion dollars in annual sales
(www.dell.com).

It is very hard to separate Dell, the individual, from Dell, the corporation. They are essentially one in the same. Dell, the company, has only
had one CEO for 17 years, Michael Dell. Therefore, to understand Dell as
a corporate leader it is necessary to also understand the company and its
direct business operating philosophy.

The Direct Business Model

"Speed is everything in this business."
—Michael Dell

While the Dell name is clearly associated with computers, what made Dell a household name had more to do with the founder's direct business model than his technical expertise (although Mr. Dell certainly has plenty of the latter). Dell perfected the direct sale computer business that is based upon a low inventory, build-to-order philosophy. This approach has a number of distinct, yet interrelated, advantages over the competition.

No Middleman

By going direct, Dell has eliminated the middleman function by being both the producer and the retailer. This means that Dell does not have to deal with an extensive distribution and retail system that, according to Michael Dell, only serves to add time and cost to the process. In the traditional production-wholesale-retail distribution system that includes warehouses, the time to market can be significant. In the computer business where obsolescence is a serious issue, the time it takes to get the product to the customer can be a competitive discriminator. Eliminating the middleman facilitates what Michael Dell says is a key to his company's success: "velocity, squeezing time out of every step in the process" (McWilliams, 1997).

Low Inventories

The build-to-order model allows Dell to keep its inventories (finished goods and parts) at a minimum. Since a computer will not be built until there is an order, there is almost no finished goods inventory to deal with. Actual customers (as opposed to forecasted ones) provide Dell with information about what they want to buy and when they want to buy it. This information is then relayed on to Dell's suppliers. In contrast, the competition's computers could be sitting on shelves gathering dust (and getting obsolete) for months at retail outlets across the country. This also means that the inventory carrying costs for Dell are far below that of the competition.

Holding inventory is very risky in the computer business because of the rapid obsolescence of the parts. The value of the inventory can depreciate by as much as one percent per week (Smith and de Llosa). To mitigate this problem, Dell keeps a minimal level of component parts on hand.

Dell is successfully able to operate with just six days worth of inventory. This compares with 60 days for the competition. The inventory advantage means that Dell can beat its rivals' prices by as much as 10 to 15 percent (McWilliiams, 1997).

Perfect Market Information

Market forecasting is a very imperfect science that can have serious consequences if any of the assumptions prove to be faulty. Many of Dell's competitors rely on sales data from their wholesale and retail outlets to determine what the customers want. With this information they decide which computers to build and in what quantity. This data has a major flaw: it's old information and it may become distorted as it comes back through a lengthy distribution system. Customer preferences are very diverse and the technology changes too fast to make an accurate market forecast. Dell's direct model effectively eliminates the need to second-guess the market.

Because Dell is in direct contact with its customers, it is able to immediately see shifts in their preferences. Because of this, Dell likes to say that he has "perfect market research." With this perfect information, Dell only builds the computers that the customers want.

Most Current Technology

It is a given that technology changes very rapidly in the computer business. It is also a given that customers want the latest and greatest in their machines. This presents quite a dilemma for a computer manufacturer. They really cannot start to introduce new technology until their (soon to be) obsolete and slow-moving machines are substantially reduced from the extensive distribution pipelines (Einstein, 1997).

Since Dell does not even order parts for a computer until an order is placed, only the most current technology gets incorporated. Michael Dell says that his direct-sell benefits his customers in two very important respects. First, the parts in his computers are, on average, 60 days newer than the parts in a competitor's computer (McWilliams, 1997). Secondly, because the cost of components declines over time in the computer industry, Dell can provide a cost reduction to its customers. This means that Dell's customers get better technology in their computers and they pay less for it when compared to the competition.

Customization

Since every Dell system is built to order, the customers get exactly, and only, what they want. At retail stores, customers rarely find exactly what they want. The features that they want may exist across three different computers but there is not one computer that has everything that they want. In this situation, the customer has three choices: 1. Wait for the next shipment to come in (maybe next week); 2. Buy the model on the floor that most closely matches their ideal; or 3. Go somewhere else. Because Dell allows his customers to order exactly what they want without any special customization charges, he tends to have very satisfied customers

Dell and the Internet

> *"The Internet will become as fundamental to your business as electricity."* (Cringely, 2001)

While many "Dot.com" companies have had a hard time making a go of it, Dell has been extremely successful in selling its computers directly over the Internet. Dell was an early advocate of using the Internet for selling. In 1996, Dell had $1 million in sales per day over the Internet. Two years later, online sales had risen to $14 million per day. Prior to the 2000-2001 industry-wide slowdown, Dell was selling $50 million worth of computers a day through its website (E.biz 25). This accounts for an incredible 50 percent of the total sales. Today, Dell is the largest online seller of computer systems in the world.

According to Dell, "The Internet is the ultimate direct model." The bottom line advantage of online sales compared to sales made over the phone can be seen in the number of people involved. To sell 50 percent of the computers through the Internet, Dell only needs a staff of 30 people. To sell the other 50 percent over the phone, Dell needs over 700 sales representatives to handle the calls (McWilliams, 1997). "For instance, order status calls, which can cost up to $13 a call, can be handled over the Internet for essentially no cost at all" (Dell, 1999).

In addition to handling sales, the Internet is responsible for handling about 75 percent of Dell's technical support. Service inquiries that would normally take place over the phone can now be taken care of by using the Internet. Customers find that it is easier to get information from Dell's website than it is to get the information by phone. This works out very well for Dell as well because Internet support is very inexpensive relative to support over the phone. Customers visit the technical database on Dell's website 400,000 times per week. There are also 160,000 file downloads every week. The 45,000 e-mail inquiries can be handled more efficiently than phone inquiries (Dell, 1999).

The Dell Customers

When we think of computer sales, we normally think of the individual PC buyer. This, however, is not the typical Dell customer. Dell specifically targets the large corporate, government and institutional customers and not individual customers. Approximately two thirds of Dell's revenue comes from sales to medium and large organizations. The other third of the revenues come from small businesses and individuals (Who We Are). The individual PC buyers only make up 20 percent of Dell's market (Cringely, 2001).

For large corporate customers, Dell establishes a custom web page tailored just for them. This feature makes it very easy for the first time Dell customer to become an ongoing Dell customer. These corporate specific web pages contain information about Dell systems the customers may already have or might want. The process for follow-on sales becomes highly simplified because many of the time-consuming administrative issues, like billing, pricing, computer configuration, and service have been prearranged. As a result, it becomes very easy to order additional computers online.

Individual PC Customers

Of those individuals who buy direct from Dell, either by phone or through the Internet, most have far more technical savvy than the average PC customer at a retail store. In other words, these customers already have a pretty good idea of what the products are all about and what they specifically want. This is especially true for the online buyer. They obviously already know how to use a computer by the fact that they are purchasing it from a computer. This arrangement has the additional benefit of screening out the problem customers who tend to be the more technologically-challenged. Michael Dell realizes that there is a built in reluctance to buy such an expensive piece of equipment sight unseen over the phone or Internet. To compensate for this concern, he made quality a major criteria in his products. The emphasis on quality (plus the absence of whining computer-illiterate customers) resulted in Dell computers receiving very high marks from the various PC, computer, and IT trade publications. As a result, Dell computers have a very positive reputation with consumers.

The Dell Company

In the very competitive computer business, Dell has 16.4 percent of the U.S. market. The leader is Compaq with a slightly larger share of 16.8 percent. If you look at all computer sales worldwide, Dell is the leader with sales in excess of $32 billion a year. This places Dell at number 48 of the Fortune 500 companies and at number 154 on the Fortune Global 500 list. Globally, the corporation has a workforce of over 38,000 in 170 countries. While most of the sites deal with customer service, marketing and distribution, there are only six manufacturing locations. There are six build-to-order sites, two in the U.S. and four overseas. The two American plants are in Austin, Texas and Nashville, Tennessee. The Texas facility, technically in Round Rock, a town north of Austin, also serves as the corporate headquarters. The four overseas sites are in El Dorado do Sul, Brazil, Limerick, Ireland, Penang, Malaysia and Xiamen, China (www.dell.com).

Michael Dell as a Corporate Leader

Dell's Business Philosophy: *"The customer drives everything the company does."* (Cringely, 2001)

Michael Dell's leadership style has been strongly influenced by the early years of his company. He worked very hard in the beginning (and he still does today). He also expects his employees to have the same work ethic. In the first few years, Mr. Dell was both the technical expert and the CEO for his company. This was fine as long as the company was small. However, this became a problem when his company approached the 10-figure mark in sales. Having been with the company longer than anyone else, he had more corporate knowledge than anyone else. Therefore, it is not surprising that he might be accused of being a micromanager. In fact, *Worth* magazine calls him the "Legendary Micromanager." He is fascinated with all aspects of his business. This includes an incredible knowledge of all the strengths and weaknesses of his products plus those of the competition. Because of his obsession for detail, he has been accused of having trouble delegating. It was not until February of 2001 that he made two of his senior managers co-Chief Operating Officers (Cringely, 2001).

His tenure as CEO has not been problem free. There have been a number of setbacks in the company's 17 years. Most of these can be traced to just two areas. The first had to do with growing pains. The other had to do with deviations from Dell's direct business model.

The way that Dell handles most of his problems is to go out and recruit the very best people that he can find that have expertise in the targeted area. After a period of phenomenal early growth, Dell had to suddenly deal with a period of negative cash flow and falling stock prices. To remedy this situation, he supplemented his staff with talented managers with proven track records from such companies as GE, Motorola, Sun Microsystems, IBM, and Western Digital (McWilliams, 1997).

> *"I think the biggest thing that I've focused on is hiring talent and surrounding myself with as many bright, capable people as we possibly can inside our business to help it grow."*
> —Michael Dell

This approached worked and the situation turned around. The company again had record profits and even higher stock prices. As a result of this experience, Dell is now very cognizant of the problems associated with uncontrolled growth:

> *"We have been careful not to grow faster than our ability to support our customers."* —Michael Dell

The company is now divided internally into more manageable groups that focus on a unique customer requirement. Each group is directly accountable for the needs of its respective customers. As a guideline, growth is seen as a problem if it impacts Dell's capacity to provide high levels of product reliability and customer service.

Although Dell is a strong advocate of his direct model, that does not mean that he did not at times deviate from his game plan. This is, unfortunately, what got him into trouble. For a brief time, Dell was selling his computers using retail outlets such as Staples and computer superstores (Cringely, 2001). This venture into the retail market was soon abandoned because it did not work. In Dell's words: "We couldn't make any money doing it" (Radosevich, 1997).

In 1988, Dell had his initial stock offering which raised $30 million. Dell used $10 million of this to develop an advanced computer called "Olympic." The intention was to have a computer that would be technologically superior to those of Compaq and IBM (Cringely, 2001). Unfortunately, this failed because it was an attempt to second-guess the market. Dell had become highly successful by having the customer tell him what to make. In the case of the Olympic computer, Dell was attempting to tell the customers what to buy.

As stated earlier, one of the major advantages of the direct model is low inventories. In 1989, Dell built up a large inventory of extra memory chips. This was done in anticipation of an expected shortage. There is unfortunately a danger in holding large inventories of computer parts. As time goes on, they typically drop in price. This is, in fact, what happened. To make the situation even worse, the entire industry was transitioning from 256-kilobit chips to 1-megabyte chips (Cringely, 2001). So not only had the chips gone down in price, they had also become obsolete.

Dell's initial efforts to develop their own version of the notebook computer did not go well. Dell decided to cancel much of what had already been developed. This action, in part, contributed to the company's first quarterly loss in 1993. To remedy the situation, Dell did what he does best. He went out and hired the best people he could find to fix the problem. This time he got his expertise from the people who designed Apple's Power Books.

Dell's Recognition as a Corporate Leader

Michael Dell's success as a business leader has not gone unnoticed. Those who monitor corporate America closely like what they see in Dell. Here are some of the accolades bestowed on Mr. Dell:

"Chief Executive of the Year"—*Chief Executive Magazine*

"Entrepreneur of the Year"—*Inc. Magazine*

"Top CEO in American Business"—*Worth Magazine*

"CEO of the Year"—*Financial World* and *Industry Week* magazines

"Man of the Year"—*PC Magazine*

"One of the Top 25 Managers of the Year"—*Business Week*

"One of the 25 Most Influential Global Executives"—*Time/CNN*

On the Personal Side

Michael Dell grew up in a very well-to-do family in Houston, Texas. His father was a doctor and his mother was a stockbroker. While Dell gained notoriety as an entrepreneur in college, he was actually an entrepreneur before he even went to college. At age 12, he made $2,000 in a national stamp auction direct marketing firm that he formed. Then, at age 16, "After extraordinary success selling subscriptions to the *Houston Chronicle*, he was able to buy himself a new BMW while still in high school." He made $18,000 in this venture (biography.com).

The success of his company has made Michael Dell extremely wealthy. He is estimated to be worth over $20 billion. He drives a Mercedes 500SL and he lives in a $22 million mountain-top estate (McWilliams, 1997). His home is the largest in the greater Austin area.

In 1999, he wrote a bestselling book: *Direct From Dell: Strategies That Revolutionized an Industry.*

All this wealth and fame does not seem to have had any negative effect on Michael Dell. As a marked departure from other CEOs, there are no scandals here. Michael and his wife, Susan, appear to be happily married with four children.

*"No one has a bad word to say about the guy. In fact,
they think he's just a regular guy who has built a great business that
most people really love working in."* (Cringely, 2001)

Wit and Wisdom

*"It's only a price war if you are losing money and losing market share.
We are gaining market share and increasing revenue."*
(Cringely, 2001)

*"The Internet is one of the things I'm most excited
about in our business."*

*"To prepare companies to operate at increased tempo, technology
and business managers who haven't already done so must retrain their
workforces for rapid evolution and flexibility."* (Radosevich)

*"If you're waiting for things to settle down and never change,
you're in the wrong business."* (Radosevich, 1997)

*"The objective of going to college is to learn—and I think I've learned
more doing what I've been doing than I ever could have in college."*
(Fishman)

*"I quit college to start Dell Computer Corporation, and I don't regret
that. But I would never advocate that young people today pass up an
opportunity for higher education. Unless you have an idea that's very
time-critical, it's always better to go to college if you can."*

References

Cringely, R. (2001). *Worth picks the top 50 CEOs: Michael Dell.* Retrieved August 27, 2001, from www.worth.com/ceos/10.html

Dell, M. (1999, November 1). *Building a competitive advantage in an Internet economy; Address to the Detroit Economic Club.* Retrieved August 5, 2002, from http://www.euro.dell.com/countries/eu/enu/gen/ corporate/speech/speech_1999-11-01-det-000.htm

Dell, Michael. (n.d.) *Biography.com* Retrieved August 5, 2002, from http://search.biography.com/print_record.pl?id=23311

Einstein, D. (1997). Michael Dell is revolutionizing PC sales. *San Francisco Chronicle.* Retrieved August 27, 2001, from www.sfgate.com

Michael S. Dell, Chairman of the Board and Chief Executive Officer. (n.d.). Retrieved August 27, 2001, from http://www.dell.com/us/en/gen/ corporate/biography/biography_generic_michael_dell.htm

Michael Dell. (2001. May 14). The E.Biz 25. *Businessweek.com.* http://www.businessweek.com

McWilliams, G. (1997, June 15). *Michael Dell: Whirlwind on the Web. Businessweek.com.* Retrieved August 27, 2001, from http:// www.businessweek.com/1997/14/b3521131.htm

Q & A with Michael Dell. Retrieved August 5, 2002, from http://www.dell.com/us/en/gen/corporate/michael_002_qa.htm

Radosevich, L. (1997, September, 15). Leaders of the Information Age: Michael Dell. *CIO Magazine.* Retrieved August 5, 2002, from http://www.cio.com/archive/091597/dell_content.html

Seo, D. (2000, August 31). Why is Michael Dell cashing out? *Salon.com.* Retrieved August 5, 2002, from http://archive.salon.com/business/ feature/2000/08/31/dell/print.html

Smith, L. & de Llosa, P. (n.d.). Michael Dell rocks. *Business2.com*. Retrieved August 27, 2001, from http://www.business2.com/articles/mag/0,1640,3718,00.html

Verespej, M. (1998, November 16). Michael Dell's magic. *IndustryWeek.com*. Retrieved August 5, 2002, from http://www.industryweek.com/CurrentArticles/asp/articles.asp?ArticleID=311

Who we are. (n.d.). Retrieved August 27, 2001, from www.dell.com/us/en/gen/corporate/factpack_000.htm

Michael Eisner
Chief Executive Officer
The Walt Disney Company

*"My only hope is that we never lose sight of one thing...
that it all started with a mouse."* —Walt Disney

Disney's Dream

Leadership tactics at Disney World are no Mickey Mouse game. *Dream, Believe, Dare, Do...*these were (and still are) the key elements to Walt Disney's success. When asked how to explain his success, Walt Disney once said, "I dream, I test my dreams against my beliefs, I dare to take risks, and I execute my vision to make those dreams come true" (Capodagli & Jackson, 1999, p. 63).

Everything that Walt achieved...the way he empowered his employees, his creativity and imagination, his service provided to customers and employees alike...all revolved around this simple four-pillar philosophy. In 1923, the then young Walt Disney approached his uncle with a proposition. He had an idea to advance animation to heights never before been achieved. He was able to secure $500 from his uncle, with an agreement to be repaid in cash rather than an ownership interest in the venture. Hindsight is a well-known phenomenon. Had the uncle opted for stock in the Disney Company instead of a cash repayment, the return on his $500 would have amounted to almost a billion dollars from 1923 to the present (Capodagli & Jackson, 1999).

Walt's management techniques are as valid today as they were when the company was founded. Capodagli and Jackson (1999) explain the critical elements of the Disney methodology:

- Give every member of your organization a chance to dream, and tap into the creativity those dreams embody.

- Stand firm on your beliefs and principles.

- Treat your customers like guests.

- Support, empower, and reward employees.

- Build long-term relationships with key suppliers and partners.

- Dare to take calculated risks in order to bring innovative ideas to fruition.

- Train extensively and constantly reinforce the company's culture.

- Align long-term vision with short-term execution.

- Use the storyboarding technique to solve planning and communication problems.

- Pay close attention to detail.

The Ground Floor

Hughes, Ginnett, and Curphy (1999) note that Walt Disney is a name that most people certainly recognize. His brother Roy, however, is not quite as well known. The two men were both an integral part of the Disney Empire success, yet they were entirely different individuals. Walt was the creative genius, while Roy was the "financial man." It was their complementary efforts that made Disney what it is today.

Walt was an innovator...one who enjoyed experimenting and finding new and improved ways to enhance a product. He wanted to be on the cutting-edge of animation, never to be outdone by his competition. He encouraged his staff to do the same. Walt was a gambler, always willing to take risks; Roy, on the other hand, was constantly concerned with the "bottom line."

One of the most interesting points that Hughes et al. discuss is the disagreement between Walt and Roy Disney over Walt's idea of a new amusement park. What is now known as Disneyland was initially opposed by Roy. Roy believed that it was simply another "off-the-wall idea" proposed by Walt. Because of this, Roy was only willing to risk $10,000 of studio money on the new project. Walt was forced to get the additional money needed to finance Disneyland by borrowing in part on his own life insurance.

After Walt's death in 1966, the creative stimulus no longer thrived. The management team consisted of all "Roy men," and they lacked the creativity needed to secure a competitive edge. The innovative stimulus, however, would eventually be reincarnated when Michael Eisner was appointed CEO in 1984.

The Man at the Helm

Michael Eisner was born on March 7, 1942, in Mt. Kisco, New York. He was son to Lester Eisner and Margaret (Dammann) Eisner. His father had accumulated a fortune as a lawyer and investor; and, as a child, Eisner lived in a luxurious apartment in New York City. In 1964, he graduated from Denison College in Granville, Ohio; he majored in both English and theater. Soon after graduation, he accepted a position in the mailroom at NBC television. After mastering the necessary skills with this position, he was destined to advance his career. Several low-level jobs followed until he applied to Barry Diller (programmer at ABC television). Diller hired him as assistant to the national program director in New York City. After being employed by Diller for four years, Eisner became director of program development for the East Coast.

Shortly after, in 1976, he was promoted to Senior Vice-President for prime-time production and development. Diller eventually left ABC to become Chairman of Paramount Pictures; and, it was at Paramount Pictures that he appointed Eisner as President and Chief Operating Officer. Together the two produced such box office hits as *Grease* and *Raiders of the Lost Ark*. The company's earnings increased markedly, and Diller and Eisner were recognized as two of the best in their industry (Hamilton, 1999).

In 1984 *Footloose* was released. This proved to be another box-office success. It was that same year that Diller left Paramount. Subsequently,

Eisner stunned Hollywood when he left Paramount and became Chairman and CEO at the Walt Disney Company.

When Michael Eisner took over the reigns as CEO, the Board of Directors also lured in Frank Wells to function as the company President. Frank was known for his business savvy, while Michael was known for his creative genius. The Eisner-Wells team appeared to parallel the Walt-Roy team. The two men immediately made changes within the organization. They felt the company had grown too complacent and comfortable...to the point of being lazy. Their plan was to bring a new style of management to the company (Hughes et al., 1999).

Eisner started the changes by instituting marathon meetings in an effort to generate creative ideas. His intent was to force members of the meeting to brainstorm; he wanted members to become uninhibited in expressing ideas to the group. The meetings were intense, but the results were very effective. The company ultimately regained its reputation as being the most successful and visionary in the world (Hughes et al., 1999).

Due to Eisner and Wells' efforts, Disney appeared to have reestablished the glorious "Walt days." The Disney operations were running at peak performance. The business was headed in the right direction...largely due to Eisner and Wells' visionary leadership. The future of Disney would change forever, however, when Eisner received a horrifying phone call one Sunday afternoon. Frank Wells' life ended tragically... he was killed in a helicopter crash while on a ski trip in the mountains of Nevada. Eisner as well as the entire Disney organization had suffered a horrific loss.

Celebrities from all over the world attended the funeral services for Frank Wells. Some of those in attendance included Gregory Peck, Steven Spielberg, Quincy Jones, and Warren Beatty. With his voice breaking with emotion, Eisner made the following eulogy remarks:

> I spoke more often with Frank than with any other single person over the last ten years. Over those ten years we never had a fight, never had a misunderstanding, never had as much as a disagreement. I was never angry with him—until last Sunday. And I was angry at Frank because he was not around to help me deal with this difficult situation...I miss him terribly. (Masters, 2000, p. 2)

Mr. Eisner had his work cut out for him since he suddenly had sole responsibility for running the Walt Disney Company. His greatest success was in reviving the company's movie and TV production. Under Eisner's tutelage, Disney produced (for the first time) movies that were targeted primarily toward the adult population, such as *Down and Out in Beverly Hills*; produced *Golden Girls* for television, along with two Saturday-morning cartoon series; and released old films and cartoons on videocassettes. Other R-rated movies followed, including *Ruthless People* and *The Color of Money*, which ultimately won Paul Newman his first Academy Award (Hamilton, 1999).

Eisner's success did not stop with movies and television production. He also spearheaded the revitalization of the Disney theme parks. His creativity with this division of Disney included a three-dimensional Michael Jackson video at Walt Disney World, along with a $300 million movie studio and a 50-acre water park.

As Disney's success skyrocketed, so too did the stock value. Eisner, for one, reaped considerable wealth. Movie hits in the 1990s such as *The Lion King*, *Pocahontas*, and *The Mighty Ducks*, along with *Home Improvement* on television, made Disney a $10 billion dollar entertainment magnet. Much of this success was attributed to Eisner's visionary leadership skills and abilities (Hamilton, 1999).

Dealing with Difficulties

In 1994, however, Eisner's health was not as successful as his business ventures. He suffered a heart attack and underwent triple bypass surgery. Disney was in limbo wondering if Eisner would be able to make a comeback. His unquenchable drive and energy did bring him back to work...and he came back with a renewed sense of vigor. This everlasting energy was directed this time at the Euro Disney theme park. Eisner's efforts assisted with the park returning back to the "black," by cutting costs and attracting additional investors.

In 1997, Eisner exercised stock options that brought him $131 million after taxes. Although it was his hard work and dedication that truly turned Disney around, some shareholders were less than enthused with his new 10-year contract worth several hundred million dollars. The disgruntled investors called the package extravagant, while the advocates of Eisner felt he was truly deserving of the money.

Another challenge for Eisner has been his critics. Many have noted that he does not like to share power. This attitude has resulted in some heated discussions with fellow colleagues. Additionally, Disney has a continuous entourage of groups protesting its movies, television shows, and merchandise. Finally, other companies attempt to edge their way into

Disney's market share. These challenges have forced Eisner to succeed at growing a company in an environment filled with obstacles.

"The great danger that arises out of such fast growth is that a company can sometimes lose its focus, or its mission, takes its eye off of its core competency. Not only is rapid growth a problem, but success, unless properly handled, can be toxic, too." —Michael Eisner

The "Disney Language"

In order to understand the Disney culture and many of the ideas expressed by Mr. Eisner, it's necessary to understand some of the terminology used in the Disney empire. Every business and trade has a language of its own. This "trade language" is usually expressed in terms of acronyms or technical words that have no meaning outside that particular business. The Disney language is unique in that it employs everyday words...but gives them a special meaning within the company. Some of these everyday words, along with their special Disney meaning, are as follows:

Attractions: Theme Park rides and shows.

Backstage: Areas behind the scenes not seen by Guests.

Cast Members: All employees of Walt Disney World.

Guests: Visitors to any part of the Walt Disney World Resort.

Host or Hostess: A frontline Cast Member who supports Guests' experiences through contact in the Show.

On Stage: All areas visited by Guests.

The Property: The entire Walt Disney World Resort.

The Show: Everything and everyone that interfaces with Guests, including entertainment, the Property, and Cast Members. (Taylor and Wheatley-Lovoy, 1998)

Training at all levels at Disney emphasizes "out-of-the-box" creative thinking. Leaders must encourage their Cast to emotionally connect with the Guests. This includes members who are both on stage or backstage. Eisner explains that Disney is driven by an "emotional engine," rather than by an "economic engine." He firmly believes that if the "emotional engine" is running at peak efficiency, so too will the "economic engine" (Taylor & Wheatley-Lovoy, 1998).

Secrets to Success

In the book titled *The Book of Leadership Wisdom* (1998), Eisner shares some of his secrets. He notes that due to the nature of his company's business, a constant stream of ideas that can be successfully transformed into film and television, radio and stage, and theme park offerings is essential to remain lucrative. He further explains that Disney creates products that people cannot know that they want until they have bought a ticket or turned on the television. At least one new product, and in many instances more, is introduced every week of the year. Consequently, innovative ideas are critical to the business.

Due to the innovative nature of Disney, the company must be receptive to new ideas from all possible avenues available...both internal as well as external. A winning idea is not always as obvious as it may seem. Eisner reminisces about various times in his career when the critics assured him that some of what have been considered among the all-time best television shows would never make it. These so-called failures included such smashing hits as *Happy Days*, *All in the Family* and *Roots*. What has Eisner learned from this research? Always be skeptical! Go with natural instincts...success will prevail for those with dedication and persistence.

> *"A company like ours must create an atmosphere in which*
> *people feel safe to fail. This means forming an organization*
> *where failure is not only tolerated, but fear and criticism*
> *for submitting foolish ideas is abolished."* —Michael Eisner

At Disney, the belief is that the only way to succeed creatively is to fail. Eisner is not a proponent of "yes men." He not only encourages, but demands that his employees speak their minds. He wants them to "rock the boat" and challenge the status quo. He wants all ideas conveyed. Brilliant ideas can never be realized if they do not have a chance to be executed.

Eisner's theory is that failing is good as long as it does not become a habit.

> Not long after I came to Disney a bunch of us would get together
> with our creative executives for what we called the Gong Show.

We would meet and toss ideas around...mostly ideas for television shows and movies. Anyone who wanted to could present an idea for a movie or a TV show. Rank had no privileges. Kinder, gentler versions of that particular activity live on.

For example, our flagship Disney Feature Animation...which has had a string of blockbusters...has its own Gong Show three times a year. Anybody who wants to...and I mean anybody...gets a chance to pitch an idea for an animated film to a small group of executives...There are usually about 40 presenters.

For this to work, you must have an environment where people feel safe about giving their ideas. While we do not pull our punches when people present their ideas, we create an atmosphere in which each idea can receive full and serious consideration. Yes, we tell people if we think an idea won't work. But we tell them why and we tell them how it might be improved. And, of course, we tell them when we think an idea has promise...and we pursue that promise. This doesn't mean that the executives are always right...or that we consider ourselves infallible. Believe me, nobody is always right in the film business. (Eisner, as cited in Krass, 1988, p. 440-441)

Some of Disney's greatest successes have been the result of Gong Show meetings.

Another way in which Eisner secures ideas from others is by brainstorming with people in all of the Disney divisions regarding any potential new idea for any part of the Disney Empire. This might include creative new rides and attractions for theme parks, new forms of entertainment, new expansion possibilities for The Disney Stores and the Consumer Products Division, or a new video game, magazine, book, record, etc. etc. etc. There are no boundaries to creativity at Disney.

Eisner explains his thoughts on the concept of synergy:

When you embrace a new idea, a new business, a new product, a new film or TV show, whatever—you have to make sure that everyone throughout the company knows about it early enough so that every segment of the business can promote or exploit its potential in every other possible market, product or context.

Most of you are aware, I am sure, that there is a natural synergy in the normal product cycle of a successful film. If it does well in its initial domestic run, it almost ensures later success in international distribution, domestic and international home video, network and foreign television, pay-per-view TV and cable.

In many entertainment companies, that is where the synergy and the story ends. At Disney, as a matter of course, a well-received film will also provide profitable opportunities in our theme parks—new rides, new characters, new parades, new attractions, and in consumer products—for Disney stores for Sears and others—toys, clothes, dolls, books, games—even children's television shows for our affiliates and owned television stations... (Eisner, as cited in Krass, 1988, p. 444)

What is Eisner's secret to not only survival but growth as well? The simple one-word answer is *rejuvenation*. When he and the late company President, Frank Wells, assessed the organization, they found complacency. The culture appeared content with the status quo. This type of environment was ripe for failure, and it was recognized early enough by the top brass at Disney. They believed that a creatively-driven company had to constantly renew itself, or its ideas would dry up and its competitive edge would disappear.

So we started moving our most promising executives around, exposing them to other parts of the business, increasing their responsibilities and bringing new eyes and new ideas to their new operations. All these women and men—young and younger, old and older—are the people who make the company work. It is top management's job to make sure they are excited about that work, and constantly renewed in spirit.

There is an old proverb that says: "If you are planning for one year, plant rice. If you are planning for 10 years, plant trees. If you are planning for 100 years, plant people." And to that I would add...plant them, but don't forget to move them around every seven to ten years. New eyes give rise to new ideas and opportunities. (Eisner, as cited in Krass, 1988, p. 446)

Leadership Development at Disney

Disney's leadership is an approach titled *Performance Excellence*. The intent is to connect leadership behaviors to the fundamental and quantifiable measure of Disney's business: The Cast experience, Guest satisfaction, and customer loyalty. Performance Excellence is a process that attempts to cultivate exceptional leaders. These leaders view their employees as centers of creative solutions, not just as members of a team who execute what management dictates. The intent is to motivate people, develop their talents, and provide proper resources and rewards to them in order to succeed. All employees are viewed as capable of taking a leadership role in coming up with and implementing creative ideas and solutions (Taylor & Wheatley-Lovoy, 1998).

Many of the Disney leaders choose to hold weekly, open-door board meetings rather than traditional closed-door executive meetings. Management generally will spend as much as 80 percent of their time in the actual Show operation...working right with the entire Cast that they supervise. Leaders willingly work frontline shifts during peak periods. The culture is the epitome of a team-based environment.

One approach utilized by various leaders at Disney is to "walk the front line." This simply means having the opportunity to experience Disney as a guest. It is an attempt to gain valuable information, such as guest satisfaction and operational performance. The leader then relays the information back to the frontline Cast Members, who can make appropriate adjustments and revisions if deemed necessary. Leaders do not withhold information; they share the information willingly with those who can implement changes to make Disney an even better source of entertainment (Taylor & Wheatley-Lovoy, 1998).

There have been internal studies conducted to determine the effectiveness of leaders throughout Disney. Based on a survey of Cast Members, the majority of Cast Members indicated pride in the organization as well as their roles within the company (Taylor & Wheatley-Lovoy, 1998). They feel that their ideas are valued as well as acted upon. Cast Members who have pride in their work are an integral part of Disney's success. The friendliness and responsiveness of Cast Members are reasons why many guests return.

Creativity at Disney

Some people think of "creativity" as a talent…a talent that some lucky people possess and which others can never attain. They associate creativity exclusively with the "arts," and they reserve the term to describe people who draw, paint, write, sculpt, or compose.

Michael Eisner does not adhere to this philosophy. He is confident that everyone has the capacity to be creative in one way or another. Everybody can contribute to the creative process by suggesting an idea that speeds or simplifies the overall process or opens up a new path for the creative process. He knows that an accountant or an administrative assistant can have a dynamite idea for a new program or product…even though they may not have the ability to "write up" or "draw out" that idea. This is the exact reason why Eisner strives to include everybody in the Disney organization in his unique "storyboarding" meetings.

Storyboarding utilizes a simple technique to solve difficult, complex business problems. It is designed to bring out the various thoughts and ideas of group participants. The process is as follows: participant thoughts and ideas are placed on cards and then displayed on a board or wall. The end result is an "idea landscape," which attempts to be more organized than the output from brainstorming, yet it retains the flexibility that project teams require as they work through the stages of problem solving and idea generation (Capodagli & Jackson, 1998).

The concept was originally conceived by Walt Disney to keep track of the thousands of drawings necessary to achieve full animation of cartoon features. Artists would pin their drawings in sequential order on the studio wall in an effort to determine which parts of a project were considered complete. This technique has subsequently been utilized in other industries as well (Capodagli & Jackson, 1998).

Another creative strategy that Disney employs is "Dream Retreats." As with storyboarding, Eisner is a strong proponent of the Dream Retreats philosophy, a concept also originally introduced by the founder of the company, Walt Disney. Dream Retreats are implemented to involve companies in needed change. The intent is to involve employees in change and enhance their understanding of the vision and direction of the company. The Dream Retreats are an attempt to prompt new ideas and innovative solutions to existing problems.

Retreats can last from three to five days. They are held at an off-site location, not within the Disney property. Off-site locations nate potential barriers to change and contribute to more effective ways to create various change. Participants of Dream Retreats are removed from their daily routine and encouraged to express their innovative thoughts and ideas.

Disney University

To be certain that employees at every level would be guided by the late Disney's beliefs and vision, Disney University was conceived. This formal training program embodies an atmosphere that is almost cultlike in nature. The training stresses the uniqueness of the company and the importance of adhering to its values. Initially, an outside firm was hired to conduct the training. However, it did not take long before it was realized 'hat people from the outside couldn't effectively convey the Disney idea ˙hospitality. From that point forward, the company recruited and trained ˙ncoming employees through what became known as the infamous ˙ey University." This internal training infrastructure was far more ˙ve than outsourcing the job, but Disney was never (and still isn't) ˙en it came time to training employees (Capodagli & Jackson,

t of the University is to train each Cast Member to embrace ˙y belief of courtesy to customers. In other words, custom- ˙ated like guests in one's home. Every new Cast Member d several days in "Traditions" training before actually ˙. During this orientation period, the Disney culture is ˙iled storytelling (Capodagli & Jackson, 1998). ˙ is costly and time-consuming, but the payoff is ˙ng Disney culture takes time and effort, but the ˙eight in gold. When guests visit any of the ˙are answered courteously, crowd control is ˙ throughout the park do whatever it takes ˙yable as possible.

and foremost task for the future is to d and anticipating the future, without ˙y of the past. This is the company's ˙ation, Eisner has vowed to be a part of

Technology is evolving at such tremendous rates, that predicting the future may only be like finding a needle in haystack. However, Eisner points out that Disney has always operated under one basic premise: people want to be entertained. This premise has not (and will not be) changed. Some theorists predict that people will engage in more and more activities that allow them to stay indoors at home. Eisner does not dispute the fact that people do have the option to do much more in the privacy of their own homes. However, Eisner also believes that the forecasters have overlooked one very important truth about human behavior. People will always have the desire to go out! There will certainly be more indoor entertainment options; but, in general, people will never desire to be totally cooped up in an indoor environment. People will always crave interaction, and will minimize isolation. Disney will remain committed to luring people out of their homes.

The Internet and digital age have also entered into the indoor entertainment equation. When it comes to creating entertainment and information of the future, and the technology to support it, Disney is covered...they now have more than 2,000 Cast Members assigned to this sole endeavor!

References

Capodagli, B. & Jackson, L. (1999). *The Disney way—harnessing the management secrets of Disney in your company.* New York: McGraw-Hill.

Eisner, M.D. (1998). *Work in progress.* New York, NY: Random House

Hamilton, N.A. (1999). *American business leaders from colonial times to the present.* Santa Barbara, CA: ABC-CLIO, Inc.

Hughes, H. L., Ginnett, R.C., Curphy, G.J. (1999). *Leadership: Enhancing the lessons of experience* (3rd ed.). New York: Irwin/McGraw-Hill.

Krass, P. (1998). *The book of leadership wisdom.* New York: John Wiley & Sons, Inc.

Masters, K. (2000). *The keys to the kingdom: How Michael Eisner lost his grip.* New York: W. Morrow.

Taylor, C.R. & Wheatley-Lovoy, C. (1998, July). Leadership: Lessons from the Magic Kingdom. *Training and Development,* 22-25.

Larry Ellison

Chairman and Chief Executive Officer
The Oracle Corporation

"IBM is the past, Microsoft is the present, Oracle is the future."
—Larry Ellison

Lawrence J. Ellison is the second wealthiest man in the United States. As President and CEO of the Oracle Corporation, his net worth is in the $50 billion range. While most people would probably be very happy with this level of success and vast sum of money, this does not seem to be the case for Larry Ellison. He has a one-way rivalry and obsession with Bill Gates. While Bill Gates is a household name, Larry Ellison is not. How can this be? Larry Ellison is the ultimate in sophistication and business savvy. If you doubt this assessment, just ask him. Larry is a bon vivant who wears $7,000 Armani suits while Bill Gates wears ill-fitting sweaters. Larry Ellison is an adventuresome and reckless playboy. Bill Gates, on the other hand, has never, ever, been accused of having such a rakish lifestyle. So why does everybody in America know who Bill Gates is, yet very few know anything about the "other software billionaire" Larry Ellison? Best plausible explanation: Life is just not fair!

The Early Years

Larry Ellison was born in Chicago in 1944 to an unwed mother who gave him up for adoption (Knecht, 2001). He grew up in a Chicago south side neighborhood. Although he attended the University of Chicago and the University of Illinois, he never graduated (this is apparently another Ellison raw nerve in addition to the Bill Gates one).

> I left school without a degree and came to California. I never took a computer science class in my life. I got a job working as a programmer; I was largely self-taught. I just picked up a book and started programming. (Morrow, 1995)

In California, he had a number of computer/technology jobs. He was the Vice President of systems development at Omex Corporation and he also worked at the Ampex and Amdahl Corporations.

Like many of the technology billionaires, Larry Ellison's success can be traced to a long-term detailed knowledge of his business, his products and a clear understanding of the market. Larry Ellison co-founded what would become the Oracle Company in 1977 (this is the same year that Bill Gates started Microsoft). The four co-founders invested $2,000 of their own money to form Software Development Laboratories. It would later be known as Relational Technologies before becoming Oracle. The initial goal of the company was to build and deliver a commercial relational database. It took two years to field the original version of Oracle before it was first sold and installed in 1979. In these early days, Larry was on the road for weeks at a time doing the installation of the software and teaching the training courses (Morrow, 1995). He has been working nonstop at Oracle ever since.

Today, the Oracle Corporation is the second largest independent software company in the world (behind Microsoft). The main office, located in Redwood Shore, California, is sometimes referred to as the Emerald City because of its blue-green appearance (guess who is called Oz?). Oracle is the world's leading supplier of software for information management. The company specializes in relational database management programs and it is also a major player in the Internet infrastructure business. Oracle's primary customers are large private corporations and government agencies. The overwhelming majority (97 percent) of the Fortune 500 companies use Oracle software.

Management By Ridicule

The success of Oracle is clearly the result of Larry Ellison's hands-on (some would say micromanagement) oversight and visionary understanding of the market. Due to his intense ambition and drive, Oracle is definitely the house that Larry built. "From the very beginning, Ellison seemed willing to do or say whatever it took to get business" (O'Keefe, 1997).

It should therefore not be surprising that the Oracle sales force had a reputation for doing anything to close a deal. Oracle had a Security and Exchange complaint in the early 1990s.

> Oracle double-billed customers for products, double-billed customers for technical support services, invoiced customers for work that was not performed, failed to credit customers for product returns, [and] booked revenues that were contingent... (Rivlin, 2000)

This case was eventually settled out of court. Oracle paid a $100,000 fine but would not admit to any liability.

Ellison is famous for his "kill or be killed mentality" toward competitors. This may help to explain why he would end company meetings with the chant: "Kill, kill, kill." Jerry Held, a former Oracle executive had this to say about the company's philosophy:

> At Oracle we don't just want to beat a competitor, we wanted to destroy them. Even when the competitor was on the ground, you kept on stomping. And then, if they were still able to wiggle a finger, you stomped on their hand. (Rivlin, 2000)

To illustrate this point, Wilson (who wrote a biography on Ellison) stated that Ellison had helped to destroy a rival software company by selling Oracle software at cost until he broke the competitor financially.

He is also willing to operate in political circles, both Republican and Democrat, if it will benefit Oracle (and Larry Ellison). He served as the co-chairman of California Governor Pete Wilson's Council on Information Technology, and he was also a member of President Bill Clinton's Export Council. He would later hire Joe Lockhardt, Clinton's press secretary, as an Oracle executive (Glassman, 2001). In the wake of the September 11th terrorist tragedy, Ellison has forwarded the idea of a national "smart" ID card that would contain such information as the social security number. This would be linked to a federal database containing digital records of the individual's thumbprint and palmprint, plus the face and eyes. The estimated cost for these smart ID cards would be $3 billion. Ellison has already met with the Attorney General John Ashcroft and with officials of the CIA and FBI. Ellison's idea was strongly endorsed by California's Senator Diane Feinstein (Ackerman, 2001).

No one would ever describe Larry Ellison as a benevolent leader. Mike Wilson, the biographer, came to the conclusion that Larry "is anything but nice." His arrogance is, in part, due to his personality, but it is reinforced by his knowledge of the industry. Having been a hands-on manager with Oracle from the very beginning, he honestly does know it all.

To get a better feel for the Ellison personality (which is totally devoid of humility), here is what has been said about him:

"Larry Ellison requires a forklift to carry his ego around."
(Consol, 1997)

"What's the difference between God and Larry Ellison?
God doesn't think he's Larry Ellison." (Wilson, 1998)

If Larry Ellison were asked to describe his management style, he would probably say "management by ridicule." "At Oracle employees are often treated as shabbily as customers and competitors" (O'Keefe, 1997). He treats everyone the same: "Friends and foes alike are verbally abused by Ellison" (Consol, 1997). A former Oracle executive who wishes to remain anonymous said that Ellison was very demanding. "When you get comfortable, and in comes a very powerful and very intelligent guy who turns over rocks and demands that problems be fixed, that can make people very uncomfortable" (Bousquin, 2000).

In an interview with *PC Week*, Ellison was asked to respond to the assertion that Oracle was a hard place for employees to work. Ellison's response: "I have no problem with asking people to leave" (Dodge and Pickering, 1995). In fact, "Ellison often fires even successful employees with little warning, and even less explanation." Many of these firings took place just before the employee became "vested." Ellison claims that when this did occur, it was just a "coincidence" (O'Keefe, 1997).

While few, if any, managerial textbooks advocate Larry's tyrannical style of leadership, it is nevertheless hard to ignore the results. Under Larry's "it's better to be feared than loved" leadership, Oracle has become one of the most profitable information technology companies in the world. This raises an interesting question. Is Oracle's phenomenal success due to Larry Ellison's unorthodox in-your-face leadership? Or, did good things happen at Oracle in spite of Larry Ellison? In other words, was Oracle simply a company that was at the right place, at the right time, with the right product?

A former senior level Oracle employee was asked this question: Is he [Ellison] a great technologist? His response: "No, there are 100 guys in the [Silicon] Valley as good as he is. Is he a good manager? No, but he's been smart enough to get them. What he is, is a great leader. His strength is to make exceptional employees do the impossible." Ellison was of the opinion that normal employees are motivated when asked to focus on an achievable goal. "However, the really exceptional people are motivated and captivated when asked to do the seemingly impossible. When talented but chronic overachievers are faced with the prospect of failure, they will succeed at the impossible or die trying" (Serwer, 2000).

Year after year, he continues to put tremendous pressure on his employees to surpass the previous year's already significant achievements. Adrian Slywotzky of *Fortune* stated that "Ellison used such get-your-undivided-attention tactics as setting outrageous, mushrooming goals for his digital initiatives." In April 1999, it was "We'll save half a billion dollars." By June 1999, it was "Make that a billion." One year later in June 2000, it was "No, make it two billion." Slywatzky concluded that these goals created a "tremendous psychological momentum."

In the mid-1990s outside analysts (whom we can probably assume are not themselves billionaires) felt that Ellison should have relinquished more of his control to the other officers of the executive committee. They concluded that Larry clearly had a problem delegating, which in their opinion was hurting Oracle. Since then he has actually increased his oversight of the operations. As a result, many members of Oracle's senior leadership have elected to move on. Chief Operating Officer Ray Lane and Executive Vice President Gary Bloom left in 2000. Lane said Ellison "pushed him out, diminishing his duties and assuming them himself." Bloom, who had been with Oracle for 14 years, felt that "there was no room left to grow at Oracle since Ellison was not going to cede the top spot anytime soon" (DiCarlo, 2000).

"If the Internet turns out not to be the future of computing, we're toast. But if it is, we're golden." —Larry Ellison

Ellison's current vision is to emulate Bill Gates' success with Microsoft's Office Suite. Just as the combined Word, Excel, and Powerpoint package was able to wipe out WordPerfect, Lotus and Harvard Graphics, Ellison plans to introduce a suite of Internet-based applications for business that tie into its database applications. If successful, this would severely undermine the products of Siebel Systems, Peoplesoft, and SAP (Serwer, 2000).

"Larrygate"

Mr. Ellison's obsession with getting the better of Bill Gates (who he calls a "convicted monopolist" and the "P.C. Pope") resulted in a major embarrassment that has come to be known as "Larrygate." During the Justice Department probe of Microsoft, a number of organizations came out with press releases, columns, and advertisements in support of Bill Gates and his company. This was apparently too much for Ellison to stomach. As a result, "someone" at Oracle set in motion a dirty tricks campaign against three pro-Microsoft organizations: the Independent Institute of Oakland, California, the National Taxpayers Union of Arlington, Virginia, and the Association for Competitive Technology (ACT) of Washington, DC.

Oracle sought the services of Investigation Group International (IGI) headed by Terry Lenzer to get the goods on the Microsoft supporters. If you need someone to dig up dirt, this Washington DC-based gumshoe firm has few equals. President Clinton's defense team turned to IGI in the Paula Jones suit. Another client of IGI was the Democratic National Committee (PBS, 1997). IGI was able to find evidence that Microsoft's public affairs and legal departments had given $200,000 to the Independent Institute. To disseminate this dirt to the media, Oracle hired the public relations firm of Chlopak, Leonard, Schechter, and Associates. The financial ties of the trade and policy groups to Microsoft were then leaked to the press without any incriminating Oracle (or Larry) fingerprints.

The President of the Independent Institute, David Theroux, said the following:

> On June 18 [2000], a guy showed up here after hours, asking for directions. The receptionist came to find me, and I gave the guy directions. But then, apparently, he came back into the office, grabbed two laptops and left. We filed a report to the police. They described it as a professional job. (Burkeman, 2000)

Is this how IGI got the information? Maybe, but Terry Lenzer of IGI would not admit to being part of this.

Unfortunately for Ellison, IGI's year-long covert operation and its Oracle connection eventually became known to the public. IGI rented space under an assumed name in the same Washington building as the Association for Competitive Technology. One of IGI's favorite investigative tactics is "dumpster diving" whereby they go through a targeted company's trash to get information. A woman working for IGI offered two janitors $1,200 for ACT's trash. They said no and reported her clandestine activity and attempted bribe to ACT.

When the lid blew on Oracle's skullduggery, Ellison immediately disavowed any knowledge of the affair. Larry said that he did not know of Oracle's involvement until he read about it in the *New York Times* (Niccolai, 2000). "I had never heard of IGI until yesterday. I never knew we were doing any of this stuff." With a reputation for being a micromanager, this "I know nothing" denial was a hard sell. When pressed by the media, Ellison changed his story. He was aware that there was an investigation underway, but he did not know what methods were being employed, or who was conducting it. Next, he admitted that he had authorized the probe but had insisted that all methods used to gather information be legal. The actual details were to be worked out not by Ellison, but by Ken Glueck, the head of Oracle's government affairs office in Washington, D.C. Ellison then said: "Did I know we were investigating Microsoft's covert efforts to unduly influence public opinion? Absolutely. Do I take full responsibility? Yes, absolutely. It happened on my watch. I authorized the funding" (Niccolai, 2000).

Ellison's credibility was sinking fast. "Some of the things our investigator did may have been unsavory," he said. "Certainly from a personal-hygiene point they were. I mean, garbage—yuck" (Cohen, 2000). He went on to say "I never knew anybody was going through people's garbage."

When the ignorance defense failed to get traction, Larry went on the offensive. He accused the advocacy groups as being Microsoft puppets working on the software maker's behalf. They were masquerading as "independent advocacy groups." "We got evidence—we proved—that these organizations—were paid for." The groups "were misrepresenting themselves as independent advocacy groups, when in fact their work was funded by Microsoft for the express purpose of influencing public opinion in favor of Microsoft during its antitrust trial."

The press was not going along with Ellison's efforts to keep the attention focused on Microsoft and its allies. They spent most of their time questioning Ellison about whether the tactics of Oracle were ethical. Mr. Ellison then had the gall to say "I feel very good about telling you about what we did." He went on to equate his "dumpstergate" activities with "civic duty." "All we did was to try to take information that was hidden and bring it into the light. I don't think that's arrogance. That's public service" (Glassman, 2001)

Here are responses from two of the targeted organizations:

"Instead of being willing to address the issues openly, Oracle has apparently felt the need to employ back-alley tactics, subterfuge and misinformation in order to achieve its aims." —David Theroux, President and founder of the Independent Institute

"It is unfortunate that instead of continuing to compete in the marketplace for database servers, Oracle and its remaining allies would rather see public choice superseded by deceit." — Jonathan Zuck, President of ACT

Microsoft weighed in with these public statements:

"This is dramatic evidence that Microsoft's competitors have engaged in a massive and ongoing campaign to unfairly tarnish Microsoft's public image and promote government intervention to benefit themselves."

"The only thing more disturbing than Oracle's behavior is their ongoing attempt to justify these actions."

Mike Wilson, the biographer, had this to say about Dumpstergate: "This was precisely the kind of goofy thing Larry might dream up." Wilson also said: "I would think Oracle's customers would want him to spend more on technical support personnel and a little less on espionage" (Girard, 2000).

Up Close and Personal

With all that money, life can get a little bit on the boring side. To liven things up, there is nothing like death defying hobbies. Larry Ellison is the owner and skipper of an 80 foot racing yacht, the *Sayonara* worth $4.3 million. In December 1998, he was one of the lucky ones in the Australian Sydney-to-Hobart yacht race. Of the 115 boats that started in Sydney, only 43 made it to the Tasmanian city of Hobart. Seven boats were abandoned, five sank, and six sailors lost their lives after a hurricane-like storm hit while the race was in progress (Knecht, 2001). Ellison had hired an all-star crew of America's Cup veterans to man the *Sayonara*. Five of them ended up breaking bones during the storm. The *Sayonara* actually won the race (for the second time). However, after the race Ellison said: "If this has been my first race I would not have gone back to sea."

If yacht racing isn't exciting enough, there is always flying. Mr. Ellison bought a $20 million MIG-29 fighter jet from the Russian government for entertainment. Unfortunately for Larry, U.S. Customs would not allow the plane into this country. The Feds didn't think that it was a good idea for individuals to have their own private jet fighter.

Larry Ellison is of the opinion that rules and laws are for other people to follow. The city of San Jose has an 11 P.M. curfew for flights in and out of its airport. Apparently, Larry did not feel that San Jose's restriction applied to him because his $55 million plane was "quieter" than most planes at the airport (Mwangaguhunga, 2000). City officials were not amused when Larry violated the airport curfew nine times. For his flagrant offense, Mr. Ellison was fined a mere $10,000. Instead of simply paying his fine, he sued the city to have the right to land his personal jet at any time day or night (Girard, 2000).

Even though Larry is a spiffy dresser, lives in a $44 million Japanese style home in California, is a world class yachtsman and drives a $350,000 Bentley convertible, this does not mean that he has class. Case in point: Hours before his third wedding, Larry asked his soon to be wife (pregnant with their second child) to sign a pre-nuptial agreement. He subsequently dumped her shortly after the birth of their child. Now divorced for the third time, Larry has no qualms about dating women who work for Oracle. During a suit with a female employee over "wrongful termination," it became public that Larry was dating three Oracle employees simultaneously (Rivlin, 2000).

On Education

Larry Ellison seems to be as obsessed with higher education (or rather his lack thereof) as he is with Bill Gates. Here is what he said prior to his commencement address at Carnegie-Mellon University.

> I'm the first non-CMU graduate to be invited to give the commencement address at CMU. And in my opening remarks, I confess that I went to a rival institution—I went to the University of Chicago—but I also confess that I did not in fact graduate, but I don't feel too bad about it, because neither did Carnegie nor Mellon. (Morrow, 1995)

His commencement address at Yale in 2000 was both outrageous and offensive.

> Graduates of Yale University, please, take a good look around you. Look at the classmate on your left. Look at the classmate

on your right. Now, consider this: Five years from now, 10 years from now, even 30 years from now, odds are the person on your left is going to be a loser. The person on your right, meanwhile, will also be a loser. And you, in the middle? What can you expect? Loser. Loserhood. Loser Cum Laude.

In fact, as I look out before me today, I don't see a thousand hopes for a bright tomorrow. I don't see a thousand future leaders in a thousand industries. I see a thousand losers. You're upset. That's understandable. After all, how can I, Lawrence "Larry" Ellison, college dropout, have the audacity to spout such heresy to the graduating class of one of the nation's most prestigious institutions? I'll tell you why. Because I, Lawrence "Larry" Ellison, second richest man on the planet, am a college dropout, and you are not. Because Bill Gates, richest man on the planet—for now, anyway—is a college dropout, and you are not. Because Paul Allen, the third richest man on the planet, dropped out of college, and you did not. And for good measure, because Michael Dell, No. 9 on the list and moving up fast, is a college dropout, and you, yet again, are not. (Warland, 2000)

If Larry Ellison's objective at Yale was to come across as a boor with no class, he certainly succeeded.

Conclusion

The Larry Ellison story can be very succinctly summarized as follows:

"This is a thoroughly distasteful human being who nevertheless managed to parlay an egomaniacal style, a hunger for wealth and power, and a cold indifference to the usual standards of behavior into colossal success and fabulous wealth." (O'Keefe, 1997)

Gary Rivlin, the author of *The Plot to Get Bill Gates,* said this of Ellison:

"Larry Ellison isn't a household name. But, if he becomes the world's richest person, that will change. He will cut a high media profile—and more people will see in his arrogance and excess the true nature of the new economy. It won't look pretty, but that's because it isn't." (Rivlin, 2000)

References

Ackerman, E. & Rogers, P. (2001, October 16). ID card idea attracts high level support. *Mercury News*. Retrieved August 5, 2002, from http://www.mercurycenter.com/local/center/id101701.htm

Burkeman, O. (2000, July 20). Silicon Valley's dirty war. *The Guardian*. Retrieved August 5, 2002, from www.guardian.co.uk/microsoft/ Story/0,2763,345291,00.html

Cohen, A. (2000, July 10). Peeping Larry Oracle's unapologetic CEO. *Time*. Retrieved August 5, 2002, from http://www.time.com/time/magazine/toc/list/0,11627,1101000710,00.html

Consol, M. (1997, January 13). The grand obsessions of Larry Ellison. *San Francisco Business Times*. Retrieved August 5, 2002, from http://www.bizjournals.com/sanfrancisco/stories/1997/01/13/editorial1.html

DiCarlo, L. (2000, December 6). Top tech execs: Larry Ellison. *Forbes.com*. Retrieved August 5, 2002, from http://www.forbes.com/2000/12/06/1206topexecsellison.html

Dodge, J., & Pickering, W. (1995, July 24). Q and A with Oracle's Larry Ellison. *PCWeek*. Retrieved August 3, 2001, from http://www.zdnet.com/eweek/news/0724/elliso.html

Girard, K. (2000, August). Dirty little secrets. *Business 2.0*. Retrieved August 5, 2002, from http://www.business2.com/articles/mag/print/0,1643,13896,00.html

Glassman J. K. (2001, March 7) Bill's and Larry's continued political misadventures. *Capitalism Magazine*. Retrieved October 1, 2001, from www.capitalismmagazine.com/2001/march/tech_bill_larry.html

Knecht, B.G. (2001, May). The proving ground. *The Colgate Scene*. Retrieved October 1, 2001, from http://www.colgate.edu/scene/may2001/knecht.html

Morrow, D. (1995, October 24) Excerpts from an oral history interview
with Lawrence Ellison. *The Computerworld Smithsonian Awards
Program.* Retrieved August 5, 2002, from http://americanhistory.si.edu/
csr/comphist/le1.html

Mwangaguhunga, R. (2000, January 22). *Insight Larry Ellison.* Retrieved
October 1, 2001, from www.macdirectory.com/Reviews/larryellison/
Index.html

Niccolai, J. (2000, June 28). Oracle CEO defends 'Larrygate.' *The
Standard.* Retrieved October 1, 2001, from www2.infoworld.com

O'Keefe, T. (1997, December 15). Inside Oracle paints CEO as prince of
darkness. *Atlanta Business Chronicle.* Retrieved October 1, 2001, from
http://www.bizjournals.com/atlanta/stories/1997/12/15/smallb7.html

Transcript of the investigators. (1997, July 31). *PBS News Hour.* Retrieved
August 5, 2002, from http://www.pbs.org/newshour/campaign/july97/
hearing_7-31.html)

Rivlin, G. (2000, May 15). TRB from Washington one of a kind. *The
New Republic.* Retrieved October 1, 2001, from http://www.tnr.com/
051500/trb051500.html

Serwer, A. E. (2000, November 1). Larry Ellison Aims for No. 1.
ABCNEWS.com. Retrieved October 1, 2001, from http://abcnews.
go.com/sections/business/DailyNews/server_talk_001101.html

Slywotzky, A. (2001, March 5). The think tank digital edge: Four
lessons from Larry. *Fortune.* Retrieved October 1, 2001, from
wysiwyg://47/http://www.fortune.com/indext...
?channel=print_article.jthml&doc_id=200622

Warland, T. (2000, July 12). *Ellison to grads: Diplomas are for losers.*
Retrieved August 5, 2002, from http://bbspot.com/News/2000/7/
ellison_grad.html

Wilson, Mike (1998). *The difference between God and Larry Ellison:
God doesn't think he's Larry Ellison.* Retrieved August 5, 2002,
from http://search.barnesandnoble.com/booksearch/
isbnInquiry.asp?isbn=068816353X&pwb=1

Andrea Jung
Chairman and CEO
Avon Products, Inc.

*"I came to Avon because I fell in love with the concept that
115 years ago, the company gave women a chance to make money
even before they could vote."* —Andrea Jung

The Young Jung

Scholars sometimes debate whether a leader is "born" or "made." It is often implied that one is a "natural leader," but it is not known for sure whether the quality of leadership can really be "natural," or whether it has to be developed and shaped by means of circumstances. Adding to this debate is the ongoing discussion about whether human beings are primarily a product of their "heredity" or primarily a product of their "environment." Or, are heredity and environment so closely interwoven that it's impossible to separate the two?

The answers to these profound philosophical questions are debatable. However, several instances have been uncovered where leaders...for whatever reason...have demonstrated some attributes of leadership at very early ages. In the case of Andrea Jung, for example, the following anecdote would seem to add credence to the theory that both heredity and environment help to determine the shape of a future leader.

When she was in fourth grade in Wellesley, Mass., Jung recalls, she desperately wanted a box of 120 colored pencils. Her parents made her a deal. She could get the set if she got straight A's in school—no B's, no A minuses, just straight A's. By her own admission, Jung was never a natural student, but she badly wanted that pencil set. So while other kids goofed around after school, Jung holed up in her room and studied. She missed out on birthday parties and tennis games, but by the end of the year she delivered to her parents a full set of A's—and in return she got a full set of 120 colored pencils. "I'll never forget that," Jung says. "My parents ingrained in me early on that the perfect score is always something to strive for. I want to win and I want to succeed no matter what" (Brooker, 2001).

The Jung Movement

Andrea Jung, CEO of Avon, attended Princeton University and graduated magna cum laude with a B.A. in English literature. Upon graduation, she accepted a job at Bloomingdale's and later moved to I. Magnin in San Francisco. She moved fast at I. Magnin and was quickly promoted to Senior Vice President and General Merchandise Manager. Her next career move was to Neiman Marcus, where she was responsible for women's clothing, accessories, cosmetics, lingerie, and children's wear.

After 10 years in upscale retail environments, Jung made the decision to go with Avon Products, Inc. as a consultant. At the time, Avon was the world's leading direct seller of mass-market beauty products, but it had begun having problems. In the early days, Avon consultants would go door to door to make the appropriate sales pitch. This approach worked fine for many years; but, as more and more women entered the workforce, fewer women were at home to chat with, and buy from, the Avon representative.

At the time Jung was recruited to Avon, sales were falling drastically, and the company's top executives were trying to combat the problem through diversification and new leadership. Their plans were not working out, however; Avon was slowly being drained of its available operating cash (Current Biography Yearbook, 2000).

In 1989 James E. Preston was selected as Avon's CEO. He vowed to return the company to its original success, and one of the ways in which he hoped to accomplish this was to bring more women into the upper echelons of the organization. As part of this process, he promoted Andrea Jung, who had been on board as a consultant for only six months, to President of the Product Marketing Group for the Unites States. This was one of the most important and most visible posts in the organization.

Jung was warmly accepted by the Avon employees. They appreciated the fact that she was a woman, and her personality was such that she easily put people at ease. She was a highly successful motivational speaker, and most of her employees...as well as the hundreds of Avon Representatives throughout the United States...regarded her as a friend as well as a boss.

It did not take Jung long to delve into action. Her first task was to get rid of the classic, stereotypical "Avon Lady" image. She felt that this image was not only old-fashioned, but somewhat demeaning. She replaced this campaign with a highly successful one entitled "Just Another Avon Lady." The new campaign not only sold products to the end customers, but it also served to enhance the image of Avon representatives. This was thus quite helpful in recruiting new representatives to work for the company. Jung also pushed for Avon to be a sponsor of the 1996 Olympics. She spearheaded an all-out effort to design a special logo, license several new products, and develop a contest in which the Grand Prize was an all-expenses-paid trip to the Olympic Games (Current Biography Yearbook, 2000). The campaign was a huge success in terms of product sales, company awareness, and employee morale.

Not content to rest on her laurels, Jung spearheaded a fund-raising campaign through which Avon Products, Inc. raised approximately $40 million to support breast cancer awareness. She also spearheaded the marketing of a successful line of women's apparel, and helped introduce the highly popular Avon Barbie doll. All of these product and promotion ideas were obviously aimed at women. They succeeded in a way that more than justified CEO Preston's decision to promote female leadership in the company...and to promote Andrea Jung to one of these leadership positions (Finn, 2001).

Jung did not restrict her creativity and leadership to implementing new ideas...she also led the team that attacked the equally difficult task of deciding which current products should be eliminated. Avon had a staple of products...each of them liked by a certain segment of the customer group. But it was obvious that many had to be eliminated. In some cases, they were eliminated because they simply were not profitable; in other cases, they were eliminated to make way for newer and more exciting products that were coming from Avon research and development. Almost half of Avon's fragrances were discontinued. She also replaced numerous makeup lines with a modestly more expensive brand called Avon Color.

The stylish packaging attracted women who, prior to learning about the new Avon line, had purchased other brands selling at higher prices. The elimination of existing products is always risky, but Jung's gamble paid off; the new product lines were soon much more successful and profitable than the ones they replaced.

Jung had complete confidence in her own instincts about the company products. She believed that Avon's niche market...working and middle-class women...could not afford such brands as Lancome or Estee Lauder. However, even though they couldn't afford those products, the desire to look, smell and feel good was still prevalent. Consequently, Jung introduced redesigned packaging to enhance the product line and make it appear as sophisticated as the product lines offered in well-known, upscale department stores.

Again, Jung's efforts paid off. In 1996 she was promoted to President of Global Marketing. Additionally, *Brandweek* named her "Marketer of the Year" in the health-and-beauty category. In 1997 she was promoted again...this time to Executive Vice President of the company. In this capacity, she was in charge of new business development. She oversaw all product research and development, market surveys, strategic planning, and joint ventures and alliances. The business press began to notice that since Jung had joined the company, sales jumped by 30 percent, profits increased by more than 40 percent, and stock prices soared 150 percent. Wall Street analysts credited Jung for much of this success, and her star was rising rapidly (Current Biography Yearbook, 2000).

Jung's seemingly unstoppable career appeared to come to a halt in 1998 when Charles Perrin, an executive from Duracell Batteries Ltd., was appointed Chief Operating Officer (COO) of Avon Products, Inc. This was a position that many industry and business leaders presumed would be awarded to Jung. Perrin's appointment to COO made some industry experts wonder if there still was a glass ceiling at Avon...even though Avon employed many high-ranking female executives.

Many people speculated that Jung would leave Avon as a result of Perrin's appointment, and that she would seek other employment in an effort to move forward with her career. But this was not the case. All speculation ceased when CEO Preston retired in 1998. Perrin was the natural successor as CEO, and Jung was appointed to COO. Then, in a surprising move, Perrin also retired a year later, in November 1999. Jung was immediately elevated to the number one position in the organization (Current Biography Yearbook, 2000).

Jung was not entirely unaware of the responsibilities and rewards that befall the Chief Executive Officer of a corporation. In 1993, she had married the then-CEO of Bloomingdale's, Michael Gould. Gould was 15 years her senior. Although she is reluctant to discuss her personal life (other than her relationship with her children), Jung later separated from her husband. She and her two children now reside in Manhattan (Finn, 2001).

Power at the Top

Andrea Jung is professional, elegant, poised, and determined to win. In many ways, she is a perfect role model for women who aspire to executive status. She is also a hard-working winner, as she was forced to demonstrate when she took over as CEO in November of 1999. The economy as a whole appeared to be bullish...yet Avon stock was bearish.

Due in large part to the increasing number of women entering the workforce, fewer and fewer women were willing or able to sell Avon products. Consequently, sales plummeted. Jung's task appeared to be insurmountable. But her persistence and tenacity would not allow her to concede. Her solution was to implement a major overhaul in just about every way in which the company conducted its business operations. She did not eliminate the "Avon Lady," rather she revived the image. As a result, more and more women were attracted to the "New Avon" and signed on as consultants.

Jung's success did not go unnoticed by Wall Street. One of the secrets of success is her uncanny ability to get to know the company. She came to Avon after working for such prestigious retailers as Neiman Marcus and Bloomingdale's. But she had no trouble adapting to the culture of Avon, which appealed to a much different, much less wealthy demographic. She did not put on airs or flaunt her past experience with upscale merchandisers...she simply accepted the Avon culture and learned to understand and appreciate the typical Avon customer.

At Avon, one of her biggest tasks was to create a global brand. One way that she accomplished this was by scrapping the time-honored slogan of "Ding-dong, Avon calling." It had been a true classic in its time, but it had grown stagnant in the minds of consumers. Jung developed a new "Let's talk" campaign to replace it.

In an effort to get an even firmer grip on the customers that Avon reaches, Jung actually became an Avon Lady for a time. She wanted a first-hand taste of what it was like to be an Avon Lady.

She later noted, "I wanted to go through the selling experience. I was going door to door in my neighborhood" (as cited in Brooker, 2001). She listened to customers' thoughts on items that had been discontinued, orders that were delayed, and just about anything else that customers wanted to share about the Avon Company, its products and its representatives. While she was keenly aware of the concerns voiced by Avon clients, she also heard many positive comments. The total of these comments...both positive and negative...continue to give her a much deeper understanding of the entire Avon business.

Due to her hands-on approach, when Jung actually took over at the helm, she was cognizant of many of Avon's shortcomings. She knew it was her responsibility to develop the appropriate resolutions to these shortcomings, and she revealed her turnaround plan to attendees at an analyst convention in 1999. She talked about her vision of developing a new line of products and making Avon available in retail stores.

Women in Leadership Positions

"In 20 or even 10 years, a 'woman at the top' won't even be a story. That will be the true statement of progress." —Andrea Jung

In September 2001, Jung took time to answer a few brief questions. The following is an excerpt relating to Jung's Fortune 500 status:

At this point, I'm one of two Fortune 500 CEOs who are women. My job has its pros and its cons. There's the opportunity to be a role model, and then there's a lot of heavy responsibility that can be very difficult. A couple of years into this role, I would say that the story is 'Andrea becoming Andrea' as much as it's Avon becoming Avon. But I'm more comfortable now with my public role as it relates to my personal life than I was two years ago. Statistics show that it's still a story when women reach the very top of the ladder, and we have a responsibility to create paths for women to succeed. What we are doing as a company is illustrating what women can achieve, and that has a contagious and inspirational effect. My advice: Just try to keep doing the right thing—and deliver.

I came to Avon because I fell in love with the concept that 115 years ago, the company gave women a chance to make money even before they could vote. When I started in marketing in the early '90s, my job was to reinvent the company's image without abandoning that heritage. Our challenge was, how do you become the Coca-Cola of lipstick? When a person wakes up in any of the 139 countries where Avon is sold and thinks makeup we want her to think Avon.

When we decided to make Avon available at retail, we wanted to introduce a brand that only we could do. Avon's Becoming is that: cosmetics, skincare, fragrance, nutritional supplements, Becoming Mom products for mothers-to-be, and a line for babies—all for the 21st-century woman. Associates in stores will be able to talk to customers about products and other concerns for women, and that combination is what will make a difference. (as cited in Shea, September 2001)

To this end, Jung takes pride in the fact that the company is predominantly run by females. Some specific company statistics include the following:

- 34% of all executives and 71% of all managers are women.

- Avon Representatives (predominantly women) earn over $2 billion per year.

- Avon's 10-member Board of Directors includes 6 women.

- Begun in 1992, Avon's Worldwide Fund for Women's Health has raised over $100 million to date.

- Avon sponsored the Avon Running Global Women's Circuit with 27 events and 12 countries in 2001 (Corporate fact sheet, 2001).

The above accomplishments are obviously very important to women, but Wall Street is more concerned with the company's financial accomplishments. And, under Jung's leadership, the company has done quite well financially. The following statistics prove this:

- Compounded annual total return for the five years ended 2000 was 23%, outpacing the S & P 500 at 18%.

- Twelve consecutive years of sales and earnings growth.

- Eleven consecutive years of dividend increases.

- Two-for-one stock splits in 1996 and 1998.

- Active share repurchase program.

- Strong cash flow; single-A credit rating. (Corporate fact sheet, 2001)

Vision

One thing that all leaders seem to have in common is a sense of vision...an insight into where their company or organization is going, and what it will take to get there. Andrea Jung is no exception. She defines the Avon vision in clear and concise terms:

> Our vision is to be the company that best understands and satisfies the product, service and self-fulfillment needs of women globally. Our dedication to supporting women touches not only beauty—but health, fitness, self-empowerment and financial independence. (Avon, 2000)

The "New and Improved" Avon

With her vision firmly in place, Jung worked at lightning speed to rejuvenate Avon, Inc. In 2000, she added 46% to Avon's research and development budget. Traditionally, it took Avon at least three years to develop a new product. Jung pushed this time frame to two years.

She set goals for herself and for the company...goals that she knew would be measurable, attainable, and challenging. One of these goals was to develop new products within the existing product line, and the company succeeded in developing several...including a revolutionary new product that was a huge success. The product was named Retroactive, and it was an anti-aging skin cream (Brooker, 2001).

Another of Jung's goals was to expand Avon's product offerings with new products that were exciting and different...yet within the confines of the vision and goals that she had described for the company. These new products included vitamins, jump ropes, yoga mats, and aromatic therapy oils.

One of Jung's most significant leadership moves was to sell Avon in retail stores. She launched a line of makeup and skin cream that was intended to sell exclusively in J.C. Penney stores across the nation. This change from the existing business model met with mixed emotions from the sales representatives. While many of the representatives were in favor of the change, others saw it as a threat to their personal business, and were angry with Jung for introducing a new distribution channel for Avon products. Jung soothed these angry representatives by assuring them that the retail line of products would be completely different, more expensive, and not a direct threat to the existing customer base.

The new, more upscale version of Avon was called "Avon Gold," and the line was introduced into the J. C. Penny stores as a completely new collection. The Avon Gold collection sported distinctive new packaging, and was priced at a level that was less than most department store brands, yet significantly higher than Avon's basic product line. For example, an Avon lipstick brand might be priced at $3 to $4, while the Avon Gold lipsticks were priced at $6 to $8 (Klepacki, Grossman, Born, Brookman, & Ryan, 2000).

To help avert potential problems from Avon's existing sales representatives, Jung pledged to keep many of Avon's most popular items...such as Skin So Soft lotion...exclusive to the catalogs traditionally used by Avon representatives. The whole idea of offering a separate distribution channel was a very sensitive issue...but Jung handled it in a way that most people agreed was as tactful and diplomatic as possible.

"Leadership"

Leadership often requires making difficult decisions...decisions that are sometimes unpopular with employees and other company executives. One sign of an exceptional leader is the ability to make these necessary changes without permanently alienating the staff, nor functioning as a dictator rather than as a leader. Andrea Jung seems to have this ability, and the Avon representative network currently seems to be as strong and as well motivated as it was before the retail distribution network was established.

When Jung took over as CEO, Avon's manufacturing and distribution systems were less than desirable. In fact, the sales representatives were still writing out their orders by hand. Jung requested that Susan Kropf, a 31-year veteran of the company, be in charge of reorganizing the process. Again, the goal established by Jung was certainly challenging, but Kropf rose to the occasion. She cut back on Avon suppliers and automated everything that occurs from the moment an order is placed to when it leaves the warehouse. Additionally, she was able to re-negotiate freight rates. Through this change alone, the company cut $400 million in costs (Brooker, 2001).

Jung's next move was to motivate the Avon Ladies. In an effort to recruit representatives, Jung reinstated a concept that was actually already in place, but was simply never utilized. The concept was titled "Leadership," and the intent was to pay existing Avon Ladies to recruit new Avon Ladies.

The rewards for the recruiting representatives were lucrative. They were granted a percentage of the sales of every new representative...as well as every representative that the new hire could recruit. Indeed, there was a ripple or domino effect that paid big dividends to those who participated in the program. Through this extremely effective campaign, Jung was able to secure a much larger sales force.

These newly recruited representatives were eager and ambitious and wanted to earn as much money as possible. They quickly distributed Avon brochures at their places of employment, their neighborhoods, banks, grocery stores, beauty salons, and any other conceivable location. The leadership program was thus revitalized, and it was clearly another success for the persistent Jung (Brooker, 2001).

Leadership Woes

One of the biggest challenges that Jung faced was the debut of the new Avon product line found in retail locations. The obstacle was not with the stores or the customers, but rather some of the sales representatives. As previously noted, the introduction of Avon products into the retail segment was met with mixed emotions from the existing Avon sales representatives. While some were genuinely excited that the move would create greater awareness of the Avon brand, others were concerned that the company would give consumers a mixed message...one that might reflect negatively on the representatives.

A sample of a few of representatives' feelings include:

- We have been told that the retail products will be completely different from the brochure line, but what does that convey?

- Is one line better than the other?

- This will diminish the image of representatives. (as cited in Klepacki et al., 2000)

To overcome this dilemma, Jung responded in the following manner:

We are committed to the technology and the marketing and the advertising and all the things we began to push this year against the core business. And that will all continue into the future. The core brand is the best value brand on the market at the best price. And the department store brand will be a value to department stores. (as cited in Klepacki et al., 2000)

For the most part, analysts have generally accepted and endorsed Jung's move into new directions. However some analysts have questioned if the choice of retail partners was the appropriate selection. One analyst wrote:

We view this news as marginally positive for Avon...We would be more excited if Avon had partnered with a discount retailer. They went with the weakest portion of the mass retail market. If they had gone with a discounter, their stock would have been up today. (Tepper, as cited in Klepacki et al., 2000)

Jung discounted this argument by noting that the decision to go into the retail market came after "An extensive amount of research and a lot of thought with the selection...the concept was first about the brand and second about the partner" (as cited in Klepacki et al., 2000).

Jung is now focusing her products into the retail segment, something that the company had historically avoided for fear of competing against its reps. A pilot of kiosks based in shopping malls is enticing younger customers who previously never purchased Avon products. In addition, she has started selling products via the World Wide Web...that opens up another new distribution channel and another set of management obstacles.

The World Wide Web is a double-edged sword for Jung. She knows that the use of this medium is undoubtedly going to increase sales. Yet her task is to decipher where her existing representatives would fit given this new way of conducting business. Her plan is to continue to keep the Avon Ladies as an integral part of the selling equation. These sales reps have been the backbone of the organization, and Jung is fully cognizant of this fact. Today, reps still produce 98% of the company's revenue, though the 80/20 rule prevails at the organization...the top 20% of the producers account for about 80% of sales. "If we don't include them in everything we do, then we're just another retail business and just another Internet site, and I don't see the world needing more of those," says Jung (as cited in Byrnes, 2000).

How does Jung plan to enter the new millennium and continue to appease her reps? She has an ambitious plan to offer her employees. She is offering existing reps more business on the Net and more ways for them to better manage the new reps whom they recruit. For a fee, any Avon representative can become what the company calls an *eRepresentative*. This is a person who can sell online, and earn commissions ranging from 20% to 25% for orders shipped direct and 30% to 50% for the orders they deliver. This form of selling benefits both the representative and Avon Products, Inc. The traditional, antiquated way of selling costs Avon approximately 90 cents to process an order. On the Web, that cost is only 30 cents (Byrnes, 2000).

Although it appeared that the Net would be an obvious move for Avon, the company was late getting started with its website. It was 1997 before the company developed a somewhat primitive website that offered just a small representation of its products. As the significance of the Web became better known, however, Avon realized that it needed to enhance the company website. An internal battle as to how they should proceed with the site prevailed. In the interim, three years elapsed…and Avon eventually lost its early online lead.

Furthermore, as executives debated the construction, usage and outcome of the new-and-improved website, representatives reacted with outrage when Avon printed the company's Web address on the catalogs distributed by representatives in their respective locations. They also criticized Avon for selling online, while prohibiting representatives from setting up their own sites.

True to her nature, Jung responded to her representatives' concerns. She mandated the company poll the representatives regarding the website…asking them specifically what type of technology would be of assistance. She then ordered focus groups to help make the site more "user friendly." Her efforts ended in a web design that provided customers with an option to shop with Avon directly, or via an *eRepresentative*.

> I don't believe [that] in the future, sitting alone in front of the Internet is how people are going to conduct their lives. What we do is about relationships, affiliations, being with other people. That is never going to go out. (as cited in Byrnes, 2000)

Arguably Jung's greatest setback was the September 11, 2001, terrorist attack on the United States. As with most other industries, the attack has taken a significant toll on Avon. The stock price dipped 10% after the attack. Jung's strategic plan to overcome this setback is quite simple: stick to the original plan. As she told Brooker (2001), "I'm not changing any of our thinking. This turnaround is far from complete. I'm probably thinking that we need to be even bolder and faster."

The Future of Avon

Jung's leadership capabilities as well as her charismatic image are critical if her expansion goals are to come to fruition. Her vision is to develop the company into offering an entirely new line of products and services, including new nutritional supplements and vitamins. Jung is an advocate of multilevel marketing...a process whereby representatives are granted a percentage of the sales of any new representatives whom they recruit. Additionally, Jung has launched *Beauty Advisor*, which trains and develops Avon representatives as personal advisers to their customer base as to what products look and work best for them (Byrnes, 2000).

Jung's vision doesn't stop here, however. She envisions that, down the road, the company will expand to include in-store spa facials and massages. At its most extreme end, Jung would like to have Avon considered a full-service company targeted exclusively at women...replete with expert financial services and legal advice as well as beauty products.

Is this taking the business too far? Some industry experts would argue yes. But Jung, true to her entrepreneurial instincts, is not listening to the naysayers. She insists that moving fast and staying contemporary is vital to securing and keeping a competitive advantage. So far, her instincts have paid off.

References

Avon. (2001). *Corporate fact sheet.* New York. Retrieved on
December 17, 2001, from http://www.avon.com

Brooker, K. (2001, October 15). It took a lady to save Avon. *Fortune, 144*
(7), 202-208. Retrieved December 11, 2001, from ProQuest Direct
database on the World Wide Web: http://proquest.umi.com

Byrnes, N. (2000, September 18). Avon: The new calling. *Business Week,*
3699, 136-148. Retrieved December 11, 2001, from ProQuest Direct
database on the World Wide Web: http://proquest.umi.com

Current Biography Yearbook. (2000). New York: The H.W. Wilson
Company.

Finn, R. (2001, May 10). Spearheading a marketing makeover at Avon.
New York Times, p. B.2. Retrieved December 11, 2001, from ProQuest
Direct database on the World Wide Web: http://proquest.umi.com

Klepacki, L., Grossman, A., Born, P., Brookman, F., & Ryan, T. (2000,
September 22). Avon's retail move: Savvy or shortsighted? *WWD.*
Retrieved December 17, 2001, from InfoTrac database (BusinessFile)
on the World Wide Web: web5.infotrac.galegroup.com.

Shea, C. (September, 2001). Avon's lady. *Harper's Bazaar,* (3478), 244-
246. Retrieved on December 17, 2001, from ProQuest Direct database
on the World Wide Web: http://proquest.umi.com

Philip J. Purcell
Chief Executive Officer
Morgan Stanley Dean Witter

Beating the Odds

Philip J. Purcell was born on September 5, 1943, in Salt Lake City, Utah. He displayed no excessive genius as a youngster; but, as he grew older, he steadily evolved into a compulsive overachiever. He earned stellar grades at the University of Chicago's business school. His stellar academic performance continued as he completed his MBA degree at the London School of Economics.

From his youth, he was raised as a Catholic. His Catholic upbringing set him apart from his predominantly Mormon peers. Even though his religious affiliation was different from the majority of his friends and associates, he remained a devout Catholic. Perhaps this early "outsider" experience helped because, at different points during his career, he has been considered an outsider; and his abilities were doubted by many analysts. At various times during his career he was "written off" by the experts, but he defied all odds and eventually became Chief Executive Officer of one of the world's most prestigious investment banks, Morgan Stanley Dean Witter ("Class meets," 1997).

101

What were the keys to his success? Biographers and business writers cite several things, but the traits most commonly mentioned include:

• Purcell always developed a vision and stuck to its principles.

• Purcell was always a strong advocate of delegating operating authority to his various line managers.

The Career Chronology

In 1967, Purcell joined McKinsey & Co. Nine years later, at the age of thirty-two, he became the firm's youngest managing director. Two years later, in 1978, the young corporate executive decided to move to Sears Roebuck & Company.

At first, his personality seemed to clash with the styles of the men who operated the large bureaucratic Sears Roebuck organization. Yet Purcell ultimately developed into one of the company's key strategic developers. Along with then Chairman Edward R. Telling, he pioneered and revolutionized the idea of Sears selling financial services to Middle America.

This ultimately led to the Sears acquisition of Dean Witter…a leading financial services firm. Wall Street was stunned by this bold acquisition by normally conservative Sears, and stunned once again, in 1985, when Sears launched the Discover Card, which targeted individual investors ("Class meets," 1997). Philip Purcell was seen by most experts to be the guiding force behind both of these bold Sears moves.

In an effort to give Purcell operating experience, Sears offered to put him in charge of the Dean Witter brokerage business. This was a difficult assignment for Purcell to accept, since it meant splitting his time between New York headquarters and the Chicago home where his wife and seven sons resided. After a great deal of consideration, however, he did accept the promotion…knowing that it would be an important stepping stone along his career path.

The "Best Team"

In 1995, Sears and Dean Witter Discover decided that it would be best for both entities if the financial services firm were to be split off from the parent company. Negotiations thus began to form a joint venture between Dean Witter Discover and the prestigious firm of Morgan Stanley. During this complicated procedure, Purcell developed a relationship with Richard Fisher, the CEO of Morgan Stanley, along with his protégé, John J.

Mack. Mack, who was an up-and-coming executive under the guidance of Fisher, was scheduled to become the CEO of Morgan Stanley in June of 1997.

After considerable discussion concerning an attempted joint venture, it was decided that a full-blown merger was what was actually appropriate.

> *"It will be more gray and rainy for some of our competitors."* —Philip J. Purcell

The complicated negotiations that occurred between the two firms is not clear, but Philip Purcell, age 54, emerged as CEO and John Mack, age 52, emerged as President. Mack was asked about his loss of the CEO position, and said, "Is it hard for me? Sure. But the point is, I would much prefer to be on the best team" (Spiro, 1997).

Mack was, however, slotted to be an integral part of the executive team. Most of the firm's business reported directly to him. Specifically reporting to Mack were the investment banking, fixed-income, and equities divisions; as well as Dean Witter's retail brokerage operation, Morgan Stanley Asset Management and Van Kampen American. Only the Discover and Intercapital divisions reported to Purcell.

> *"To me, a great company is defined by the fact that it is not compared to its peers."* —Philip J. Purcell

Investors seemed to be receptive of the merger. Morgan Stanley's stock gained 7 1/8 points on the news. The belief among investors was that the two firms would be able to generate more business together than they would be able to generate individually. Dean Witter brokers would have more products to sell, given Morgan Stanley's strength in international money management and underwriting. Morgan Stanley would win more underwriting mandates, since it would now have greater retail distribution through Dean Witter's network of 9,300 brokers (Spiro, 1997). It seemed to be a match made in Heaven, because Dean Witter was popular with small investors, while Morgan Stanley flourished with large institutional clients.

A Deal Gone Sour

When the $10 billion merger occurred, Dean Witter's Mr. Purcell was appointed Chairman and CEO. Some people predicted immediate trouble because Morgan Stanley insiders owned approximately 18% of the combined company, and their counterparts at Dean Witter owned only about

6.8 percent. Many Wall Street gurus believed that Mr. Mack would soon oust Mr. Purcell from the top seat. Much to the surprise of the experts, this never happened. In fact, the newly formed company of Morgan Stanley Dean Witter seemed to function smoothly and thrive financially.

It was later rumored that, in the summer of 1998, Mr. Mack approached Mr. Purcell regarding the possibility of becoming a co-CEO of the organization. According to the rumor mill, this idea developed after co-chief executives were established at Citigroup in April of 1998. Mr. Mack supposedly bounced his idea off Richard Fisher, his mentor at Morgan Stanley and a current influential board member, who brought it up at a subsequent board meeting.

At the time, a Morgan Stanley spokesperson attempted to minimize the effect of the rumor with the following comment:

> Mr. Mack and Mr. Purcell did discuss the merits of a co-CEO structure—but they mutually agreed that such a structure would not provide a better platform for the management of our company. It would be wrong to characterize those discussions as a power play, or to indicate that Mr. Mack was rebuffed. (Smith, 1999)

In reality, Mr. Purcell had armed himself in advance against this potential threat. When the merger was negotiated in January 1997, Mr. Purcell had demanded a provision that required a three-quarters vote of outside directors to remove Mr. Purcell or Mr. Mack (or modify either of their respective roles, duties, or authority) (Smith, 1999).

A senior executive in favor of keeping Mr. Purcell at the helm noted that the two top men were already running the firm jointly, and that directors generally wanted to know clearly "who's on the line if something goes wrong" (Smith, 1999).

All internal rumors and politics were put aside when a disaster involving an emerging-markets bond fund overseen by Morgan Stanley executives suddenly emerged. The fund was overloaded with Russian debt when Russia devalued the ruble, and subsequently defaulted on its debts. The fund lost substantially, and Morgan Stanley Dean Witter had pretax bond losses of approximately $300 million. These losses tarnished Mr. Mack's reputation...particularly because a good percentage of the losses were in the pension fund of a large corporate client. Three Morgan Stanley executives with oversight responsibility for the fund resigned (Smith, 1999), but Mr. Mack still received much negative publicity.

Scandals at the Newly Merged Company

In addition to world market problems, scandals also erupted within the corporation. According to Wirth (2001), there were several scandals that tarnished the reputation of the company. The first involved the firing of Christian Curry, a junior analyst in the firm, after nude pictures of him were published in a gay pornography magazine. Morgan Stanley Dean Witter told the press that Curry was fired for "padding" his expense report, but Curry didn't accept the accusation and filed a $1.8 billion racial and sexual orientation discrimination lawsuit against his employer.

Moreover, it was revealed later that Morgan Stanley had paid another individual $10,000 to entice Mr. Curry into planting racist e-mails on the company's internal computers to bolster his lawsuit. A top legal official representing Morgan Stanley Dean Witter, and a personal friend of Mr. Purcell's, abruptly resigned from the company in the middle of the lawsuit. The suit was eventually settled, and a company spokesperson claimed that Morgan Stanley Dean Witter did not give Mr. Curry any type of monetary settlement. However, most people who were close to the matter believed otherwise. They felt there was, in actuality, a multimillion dollar settlement given to Mr. Curry.

During the Curry lawsuit, another scandal was brewing. In July 1999, an employee named Robert Kitts was fired for his affair with a young research assistant, Elena Drill. Several weeks later, Drill was found shot to death in her apartment. New York City Police claimed she was the victim of a murder-suicide, with a former boyfriend as the one who pulled the trigger.

The saga didn't end there. Shortly after Curry was fired, another employee filed a lawsuit. Allison Schieffelin, a saleswoman in the company's convertible securities unit, filed a suit stating she had been denied a promotion due to her gender. The Equal Employment Opportunity Commission (EEOC) agreed to hear her case. After investigating her claim, the EEOC sided with Ms. Schieffelin, indicating that she had been unjustly denied a promotion. Mysteriously, while the meetings with the EEOC were still taking place, Morgan Stanley Dean Witter fired Ms. Schieffelin. This move showed extremely bad judgment on the part of the firm and caused still another scandal in which the leadership of the company was found lacking.

The coup de grace came when the company hired former President Bill Clinton as the keynote presenter at an investor-client conference. His presentation earned him $100,000...an amount that many investors found difficult to accept. A few days after the speech, Purcell told the press that inviting Clinton to speak had been a mistake, and that the invitation had not received the proper internal review. He told the press that the company should have considered the strong feelings of clients who were not pleased with Clinton's activities during his final days in the Oval Office.

Apparently, Clinton was furious over Purcell's comments. A spokesperson for Clinton noted that the former President received a warm ovation, and Purcell's comments were not appropriate. The person who was responsible for securing Mr. Clinton, Michael Rankowitz, quit the company in a huff. A former Morgan Stanley Dean Witter employee stated that Purcell was simply trying to save his own reputation by blaming other people and trying his best to not be held accountable for any of the negative company publicity.

A Verbal Agreement

After the spate of scandals and bad publicity, tension still existed between the two top men at Morgan Stanley Dean Witter. The January 19, 2001, headlines in the *Wall Street Journal* read "Deals & Deal Makers: Will Two Wall Street Reign Makers Cede Their Thrones?—A Handshake Agreement Adds to the Tense Times At Top of Morgan Stanley."

According to the article, Mr. Mack was not content with his role at the merged organization. What surfaced was an alleged private promise by Mr. Purcell to effectively hand over the CEO position to Mr. Mack as early as 2002. This supposed "gentlemen's agreement" was reportedly made prior to the Dean Witter and Morgan Stanley merger that created the firm in 1997.

According to the story, several of Mack's top lieutenants had left the organization, and Mack was skeptical as to whether the original promise made by Mr. Purcell would come to fruition. Given the fact that the current board consisted of eight people who were once part of the Dean Witter regime and only three individuals from the Morgan Stanley side, the story seemed reasonable; and, once again, rumors began to run rampant.

This time, however, the gossip was that Mr. Mack was considering leaving the firm. Neither man...nor any official of the company...was willing to comment to the media. The loss of Mr. Mack would be a tremendous setback to Morgan Stanley Dean Witter. He had stellar relationships with many of the firm's largest clients, and a reputation of being willing to travel extensively to meet with investors and possible clients. Additionally, many segments of the organization reported directly to Mr.

Mack. One of these segments was the firm's institutional business, which accounted for more than 60% of the company's total revenues. As one analyst noted at the time:

> The loss of John Mack would be a major blow to the firm, because he's viewed as a leader inside Morgan Stanley. He personifies the firm's institutional business, which is the driving force of the company's earnings growth. (Gasparino, 2001a)

As a general rule, all mergers are difficult to consummate. But this particular one was supposed to be relatively simple. Both firms agreed initially that they would offer complementary skills. From the very beginning, the two top executives seemed off to a good start. Mr. Mack, the chief executive of Morgan Stanley, agreed to hand over the CEO position to his counterpart, Mr. Purcell. This was primarily because Mack felt strongly that the transition would create the epitome of a powerhouse organization.

Probably more importantly, there was the alleged "verbal agreement" with regard to the transfer of leadership, which ultimately gave Mr. Mack the CEO position. Part of this supposed agreement was the fact that the two men would both be working at the company for 10 years; and, that each would run the firm for half that time. However, it was not clear what Mr. Purcell's capacity would be after his five years at the helm (Gasparino, 2001a).

The Resignation

The original merger of Morgan Stanley and Dean Witter was billed as a merger of equals. Although Mr. Purcell assumed the position as Chairman and Mr. Mack the position of President, it was stated publicly that all major decisions would be made jointly by the two men. Insiders have noted that, in reality, however, this really never happened. Internally, the two men supposedly butted heads on most major decisions, and Mr. Mack had threatened to quit on numerous occasions.

As more and more people from the Morgan Stanley side left the company, Mr. Mack felt increasingly isolated. Finally, he decided it was time for him to leave as well. On January 24, 2001, Mr. Mack tendered his resignation (effective March 2001). In a news release, Mr. Mack promised the following to the company stakeholders, "I will work with Mr. Purcell to ensure that there is a smooth transition in the leadership of the company. I will assist Mr. Purcell with client relationships and commitments and in communicating the transition to our employees" (Gasparino, 2001b). In response, Mr. Purcell stated:

> No one has done more than John Mack to make Morgan Stanley Dean Witter the world's leading financial services firm. His absolute commitment to excellence and his unstinting dedication to the men and women of Morgan Stanley Dean Witter and its clients [have] set the standard by which the new generation of leaders of our firm will measure themselves. As my colleague, as a leader, and as a mentor and friend to the most talented people in our industry, he will be greatly missed. (Gasparino, 2001b)

The Impact on the Company

Although everyone made the proper statements in public, there is little doubt that there were hard feelings between the two men. It was clear that Mr. Mack felt that he been lied to at the time of the merger.

According to some insiders, Morgan Stanley's former chief executive, Richard Fisher, called Mr. Purcell to persuade him that it was a mistake to let Mr. Mack leave. He recommended that Mr. Purcell take the issue to the board to get its input. Mr. Purcell agreed to Mr. Fisher's request. However, the board, which consisted in majority of former Dean Witter people, agreed with the resignation of Mr. Mack.

The departure was seen as a blow to what many analysts considered the most successful financial-services merger in history. After the two companies came together, the stock nearly quadrupled…significantly more than the industry average (Gasparino, 2001b).

On the minds of most people close to the situation was the potential impact of Mr. Mack's departure to the financial well-being of Morgan Stanley Dean Witter. According to one analyst following the announcement, "The biggest risk for Morgan Stanley is that key people will follow his lead. I think it's a high probability and major risk" (as cited in Gasparino, 2001b).

Purcell…Alone at the Helm

Despite Mack's departure, the two men acted graciously when out in the public eye. Mack conceded to the board and asked that they protect his legacy…his shareholdings in Morgan Stanley, which were then worth approximately $488 million. Mr. Purcell appointed a Morgan Stanley veteran, the firm's chief financial officer, Robert G. Scott, to replace Mr. Mack. Additionally, he decided it was time to drop the Dean Witter name…the company would now simply be known as Morgan Stanley.

Running the organization alone was not an easy task for Mr. Purcell. One particularly pressing problem was that several of the company's key executives…most of whom had been loyal to Mr. Mack…were bailing out of the organization. Purcell was now faced with the task of operating the organization and keeping the firm running smoothly with a new management team. According to Purcell, "It's not an exodus. It's a new generation of management" (Thornton, 2001).

One of Purcell's greatest tasks in the future will be the continual bridging of the cultural differences that still exist between the once-prestigious Morgan Stanley and the more down-to-earth mass retailer Dean Witter. Purcell argues that these cultural bridges have already been crossed, and the two different cultures are a thing of the past. However, there are still many people…both inside and outside the corporation…who believe that Purcell still has to break down a few remaining walls that still separate Morgan Stanley and Dean Witter.

Purcell has initiated change. Under his command, Morgan Stanley has started to shake up its ranks. Employees were previously paid generous bonuses for securing deals or elevating the revenues of their respective departments. Purcell instituted a new program whereby compensation was based on the amount Morgan Stanley gets from the total fees each client pays to Wall Street, rather than the absolute dollar amounts of transactions. In addition to this change, Purcell has consolidated Morgan Stanley employees from various locations around New York City into a central office.

In yet another change, Purcell has developed a team composed of up-and-coming company executives. Their primary objective is to create a system for serving clients in the most efficient and effective manner possible. The team consists of many individuals with a characteristics similar to Purcell's; in other words, they are hard-driven strategic thinkers. Mr. Purcell himself claims, "Easily the most important thing I've done is pick people" (as cited in "Morgan Stanley's," 2001).

The Rumor on the Street

Persistent market rumors have it that Morgan Stanley may sell its Discover unit to another company or merge it (or the complete company) with American Express. Purcell, however, did not feel that a major transaction was necessary. "It's a fine business. With a market capitalization of $66 billion, it would be difficult for Morgan Stanley to swallow American Express, worth $55 billion" (Purcell, as cited in "Morgan Stanley's," 2001).

In these days of giant mergers, anything is possible. Morgan Stanley may well merge with another company during Mr. Purcell's time at the helm. Given his past problems with shared leadership, however, it is doubtful that he will enter into any agreement that does not give him either complete control...or any exceptionally lucrative buyout. History has shown that he will not likely share management with anyone else.

Terrorist Attacks Unite Rivals John Mack and Philip Purcell

After the terrorist attacks on September 11, 2001, two one-time rivals...John Mack and Philip Purcell...were united once again.

In any catastrophe, people tend to come together. This was true for Mr. Mack and Mr. Purcell as well. Immediately after the attack, Mr. Mack moved to offer comfort and support to Mr. Purcell. He left a voice-mail message expressing his concern for Morgan Stanley's 3,700 employees in the Trade Center and offered to help in any way possible (Opdyke and Gasparino, 2001).

One day later, Mr. Mack, who was then CEO of rival Credit Suisse Group's Credit Suisse First Boston, was at a gathering for Wall Street brokers, and Mr. Purcell was also present. This marked the two gentlemen's first appearance together in public since their bitter power struggle separation. Mr. Purcell acknowledged Mr. Mack's phone call of the day before and conveyed his gratitude for the message. The two men were gracious to each other and went on to work together to help their respective businesses, as well as the entire financial world, recoup from the devastation caused by the Trade Center attacks (Opdyke and Gasparino, 2001).

The reunion of these two men seemed to symbolize a growing trend on Wall Street: namely, cooperation and reconciliation among fierce rivals. It has been heartening to many to see how once-bitter enemies in the business world have worked together for the good of the business community after the September 11 attack. The companies who suffered the least have generously loaned people, office equipment, and computer facilities to those companies who suffered the most. Cutthroat competition will undoubtedly resume once Wall Street is somewhat back to normal, but America's leading financial companies will always be proud of the way they worked together in a time of crisis.

Earning the ELAN Award

Each year the *Wall Street Letter* (WSL) honors outstanding individuals in the securities industry. WSL readers were asked to vote for those personalities who have made the greatest contribution to their fields in 2001. The winner would be the recipient of the ELAN (Enterprise, Leadership and Achievement of Note) award. The response from readers was impressive...over 1000 votes were cast. Each nominee represents the pinnacle of his or her industry. Mr. Purcell was one of the nominees. The article notes the following with regard to Mr. Purcell:

> Purcell emerged as the firm's preeminent leader after overseeing several years of integration between its two main components, which were powerhouses in their own right: Morgan Stanley in the institutional space, and Dean Witter in the retail space. In addition, he stood tall during recovery efforts in the aftermath of the attacks on the World Trade Center, which destroyed the downtown headquarters of the Dean Witter arm of the firm. He led a massive effort ensuring that over 3,500 surviving employees who were located in the area and survived the attacks were relocated and back to work in short order. (2001 ELAN awards, 2002a, February 4)

One week after printing the nominations, WSL publicized the results: Mr. Purcell was the winner. As was printed in the program:

> After the attacks on the World Trade Center destroyed the downtown headquarters of Morgan Stanley, Philip Purcell, the firm's Chairman and CEO, jumped into action. He immediately instructed employees not to return to Two World Trade Center or Five World Financial Center after the first plane hit. Later that day, he refitted the Discover Card call center to act as a hotline for the 3,700 Morgan Stanley employees working in the destroyed buildings to call in and report that they were safe. The hotline was up and running so quickly that it became a clearinghouse for employees at other firms to report that they, too, were safe. Later, Purcell broadcast daily televised conferences to all employees.

> The immediate result was that Morgan Stanley employees were evacuated to safety, and back-up systems were up and running on September 12, with employees returning to work soon there-

after. For his cool exhibition of leadership under fire, the editors of *Wall Street Letter* have named Purcell as the winner of the publication's 2001 ELAN award in the CEO category. (2001 Elan awards, 2002b, February 11)

Purcell is a firm believer that Morgan Stanley has changed dramatically since the attacks of September 11. As he states, "It certainly ended the merger. Now, it's a tight-knit single firm. Before, it was two tight-knit firms" (*Wall Street Letter*, 2002). He acknowledges that, if there was any good that came out of the devastation of terrorism, it was his employees' resilience and courage in the face of the crisis. He proudly recounts the story of a group of employees who left the World Trade Center and went directly to the firm's back-up site on Varick Street. "These people were traumatized, and yet they first went to Varick Street to make sure they could take care of clients and other people" (2001 ELAN awards, 2002b, February 11).

A Feather in his Cap

After recovering from the initial terror and devastation of the terrorist attacks, all of Wall Street, including Mr. Purcell, tried to return to business as usual. One of the first business problems faced by Mr. Purcell was the fact that one of his senior executives was offered a top job at Mr. Mack's firm, Credit Suisse First Boston. Since Mr. Mack had already lured several other top executives for Morgan Stanley before the terrorist attacks, the loss of this particular executive would have been a severe blow.

Mr. Purcell made an aggressive counter-offer and this...combined with the new spirit at Morgan Stanley...convinced the executive to stay. It was happy moment for Philip Purcell and may well have been a defining moment in the history of Morgan Stanley under the sole leadership of Mr. Purcell.

It can now be said that Morgan Stanley is a single company, with a single leader. It is not certain where the company will go from here, but Philip Purcell is clearly the hand guiding the ship...and the credit or the blame for whatever comes next will be his alone.

References

2001 Elan awards. (2002a, February 4). *Wall Street Letter*, 34, 5. Retrieved April 27, 2002, from ProQuest Direct database on the World Wide Web: http://proquest.umi.com

2001 Elan awards. (2002b, February 11). *Wall Street Letter*, 34, 6. Retrieved April 27, 2002, from ProQuest Direct database on the World Wide Web: http://proquest.umi.com

Anonymous. (2001, February 3). Finance and economics. *The Economist*, 8207, 78. Retrieved April 27, 2002, from ProQuest Direct database on the World Wide Web: http://proquest.umi.com

Class meets mass on Wall Street. (1997, February 17). *Business Week*, 3514, 78. Retrieved April 27, 2002, from ProQuest Direct database on the World Wide Web: http://proquest.umi.com

Gasparino, C. (2001a, January 19). Deals and deal makers: Will two Wall Street reign makers cede their thrones? A handshake agreement adds to the tense times at top of Morgan Stanley. *Wall Street Journal* [eastern edition], p. C.1. Retrieved April 27, 2002, from ProQuest Direct database on the World Wide Web: http://proquest.umi.com

Gasparino, C. (2001b, January 25). Morgan Stanley's Mack steps down after rift. *Wall Street Journal* [eastern edition], p. C.1. Retrieved April 27, 2002, from ProQuest Direct database on the World Wide Web: http://proquest.umi.com

McGeehan, P. (2002, February 21). Senior executive at Morgan Stanley will remain with firm. *New York Times*, p. C.12. Retrieved April 27, 2002, from ProQuest Direct database on the World Wide Web: http:// proquest.umi.com

Morgan Stanley's midlife crisis. (2001, February 12). *Business Week*, 3738, 90. Retrieved April 27, 2002, from ProQuest Direct database on the World Wide Web: http://proquest.umi.com

Opdyke, J. & Gasparino, C. (2001, September 24). Rebuilding Wall Street: Wall Street rivals become allies. *Wall Street Journal* [eastern edition], p. C.1. Retrieved April 27, 2002, from ProQuest Direct database on the World Wide Web: http://proquest.umi.com

Smith, R. (1999, March 10). Dean Witter holds its own at Morgan. *Wall Street Journal* [eastern edition], p. C1. Retrieved April 27, 2002, from ProQuest Direct database on the World Wide Web: http://proquest.umi.com

Thornton, E. (2001, February 12). Morgan Stanley: Life after Mack. *Business Week*, 3719, 84-86. Retrieved April 27, 2002, from ProQuest Direct database on the World Wide Web: http://proquest.umi.com

Wirth, G. (2001, March 26). Checkmate: How Dean Witter outmaneuvered Morgan Stanley. *The Investment Dealers' Digest.* Retrieved April 27, 2002, from ProQuest Direct database on the World Wide Web: http://proquest.umi.com

Sumner Redstone

Chairman of the Board and Chief Executive
Officer, Viacom Inc.
Chairman of the Board and Chief Executive
Officer, National Amusements, Inc.

The Path to Success

"Whatever I've done, good or bad, in my life there's been an obsessive drive to win, to do it the best." —Sumner Redstone

Sumner Redstone was born in 1923 in Boston, Massachusetts. He was blessed with a high degree of intelligence and was accepted into the Boston Latin School, which is the oldest, and quite possibly the toughest, public school in the country. While there, he excelled on the school debate team and was the recipient of numerous academic awards.

Upon graduation, he was accepted in the class of '44 at Harvard...at the youthful age of 17. While at Harvard, Redstone became fluent in Japanese and proficient in Latin, French, and German. Professor Edwin Reischauer, who later became Ambassador to Japan, observed Redstone's skills in college and later selected him to join an elite Army code-cracking team during World War II. After the War, Sumner entered Harvard Law School and married Phyllis Raphael in 1947 (Matzer & Lenzner, 1994).

As an attorney, he served in various capacities for the United States government. In 1951, at the age of 28, he left government work and became a partner in the Washington law firm of Ford, Bergson, Adams, Borkland, & Redstone. He eventually became restless with the law firm and decided to leave law and pursue a business career. He said, "When I found out I wasn't going to make the world better by being a lawyer, I decided I wanted to be in business for myself" (Redstone, as cited in Matzer & Lenzner, 1994).

As an entrepreneur, Redstone bettered both the world and himself. He joined his father and brother in the family's business, National Amusements, which owned a chain of 12 drive-in theaters in the Northeast. A visionary, Redstone noticed trends that would ultimately reshape the movie business. People were leaving the major cities and flocking to the suburbs. Land was becoming increasingly scarce and more valuable.

Analyzing these trends, Redstone came to the realization that drive-in theaters would eventually lose their appeal, and that suburban theaters would be the wave of the future. He also pioneered the idea of clustering several screens at single indoor locations. Hence the multiplex was born…a concept that Redstone is credited with creating (Wasserstein, 1998).

Sumner was both a shrewd businessman and an intelligent investor. He cultivated the family's movie theater chain until it grew from 59 to 129 theaters…with over 800 screens. By the time he was in his fifties, Sumner Redstone was a wealthy and successful movie exhibitor and could probably have retired to a life of relative ease. That wasn't Redstone's way, however, and he worked diligently to expand his family's business.

A Near-Death Experience

In March of 1979, at the age of 56, Sumner Redstone had an experience that would have forced most men into retirement. He was trapped on the third floor of the Copley Plaza Hotel in Boston by a fierce fire that rapidly spread throughout the building. He was in the hotel because he had attended a party there to honor a branch manager of Warner Bros. Pictures. Knowing that the party would run late, Redstone booked a room and planned to spend the night. After leaving the party, he went to his room and went to bed. He awoke to the smell of smoke. In his own words:

I smelled smoke and made the classic mistake; I opened the door. The branch manager, who was staying in the next room, made a bigger mistake. He opened his door wide and stepped into the hotel corridor. He died.

I was enveloped in flames. The fire shot up my legs. The pain was searing. I was being burned alive. But even in the middle of terror there is sometimes clarity. I thought, what a horrible way to die.

Somehow I staggered to the window. It was stuck, I couldn't budge it. I moved to another window and, I don't know how, got it open and clambered outside. I was kneeling on a tiny ledge, barely big enough to put one foot on. I was three floors up. If I jump, I'm dead. Flames were shooting out of the window head-high and I crouched there, hanging onto the windowsill, my fingers cupped, my right hand and arm in the fire and burning.

I hung on the ledge for what seemed like forever. Finally a hook-and-ladder truck arrived. A fireman climbed up, cradled me in his arms and carried me to the ground. (Redstone & Knobler, 2001, pp. 15-16)

The cause of the fire was later determined to be arson…a fire started by a disgruntled former hotel employee. Redstone sustained severe burns over 40 percent of his body and underwent over 60 hours of operations that included multiple skin grafts. His right wrist was severely burned and was limp, literally hanging on his arm. Some experts thought he would never walk again, but they didn't understand what a tireless fighter he was. After spending months in the hospital and over a year of rehabilitation, Sumner slowly returned to his business endeavors.

When reminiscing about the fire that nearly took his life, Sumner says:

I had the same value system after the fire that I had before. Whether in high school or college or law school or building a theater circuit, I have always been driven. I have a passion to win, and the will to win is the will to survive.

The most exciting things that have happened to me in my professional life have occurred after the fire…but not because of it. It doesn't take near death to bring you to life. Life begins whenever *you* want it to begin. (Redstone & Knobler, 2001, pp. 20-21)

Great successes are built on taking the negatives in your life, the challenges and the frustrations, and turning them around. Taking a negative and turning it into a positive...I think I was always driven before, but out of that fire came most of the exciting things I have ever done. (Redstone, as cited in Current Biography Yearbook, 1996, p. 450)

The Deal-making Begins

After his recuperation and his return to the family business, Redstone realized that the business...now known as National Amusements...did not have that much potential for further growth. Good theater locations were scarce and movie rentals were growing at an alarming rate, so Redstone decided to "hedge his bet" by investing in the content side of the movie business. As luck would have it, he made this decision in the early '80s...just as the frenzy of merger deals in the United States was beginning.

His first few investments were small, but he started accumulating shares of Viacom in 1986. In 1997, he surprised many people in the industry by effecting a leveraged buyout of Viacom, the cable television operator that owned the music-video channels MTV and VH1, as well as the children's channel Nickelodeon. This successful buyout was the first of many.

Looking back on this first major acquisition, Redstone admits that he was somewhat frightened, because he was risking the family's asset base in a business that he wasn't very familiar with. He was "betting the ranch," and he admits it was scary:

National had only 250 screens at the time...if we borrowed $10 million it was a major event. Here we borrowed $240 million. If anything happened, it would have taken a long time to dig out a chain of 250 screens from hundreds of millions in debt. (Matzer and Lenzner, 1994)

The Hard-Fought Paramount Takeover

In 1993, Mr. Redstone set out to expand Viacom by means of an attempted acquisition of Paramount Communications. Paramount Communications' assets included the Paramount movie studio and Simon & Schuster, the publisher. It was agreed that Martin S. Davis, Paramount's Chairman, was to be chief executive of the combined company, while

Redstone would retain the position of Chairman. Under the original plan, Viacom was to take on minimal debt since the majority of the deal was financed with stock.

But a bidding war started when QVC, a cable-television company operated by Barry Diller, a former Paramount executive, entered the game. After a prolonged and sometimes very vicious and personal legal battle, Viacom ended up with Paramount…but it also ended up severely in debt. The company then issued some very unique securities, with names like contingent value rights, whose value was dependent on the trading value of Viacom stock. As another offshoot of the prolonged legal battle, Mr. Davis ended up unemployed, because the CEO role was eliminated.

In that same year, Redstone engineered a highly publicized merger with Blockbuster Entertainment, the video retail giant. Blockbuster later had some rough years, but one of its values to Redstone was that Viacom needed Blockbuster's cash flow to merge with Paramount. The whole Viacom-Paramount-Blockbuster deal was extremely complicated, and it would probably never have come about if not for Sumner Redstone's legal background and his extreme competitive spirit.

Viacom and CBS…Who's the Boss?

In 1999, the CEO of CBS, Mel Karmazin, approached Redstone with an offer. The offer was for CBS to purchase Viacom. Redstone countered with an offer for Viacom to buy CBS. The two men hashed out a deal, and the rest is history.

According to the deal, each man would be an integral part of the newly-formed organization. Though Redstone remained the company CEO and controlling shareholder, Karmazin got a three-year contract that allowed him to operate Viacom according to his own guidelines. Although the two are required to consult each other on strategic matters, Redstone is forbidden to interfere with the day-to-day operation of the business. In fact, the bylaws of the merged company contain the following unusual language, "Viacom's CEO shall not exercise any powers, rights, functions, or responsibilities of the President and chief operation officer unless Mel Karmazin is the chief executive officer" (Leonard, 2001). Karmazin defaults to the position if Redstone resigns.

Knowing that Redstone is a bit of a "control" person, many industry analysts did not think the duo could perform effectively in dual leadership roles. Since Redstone was a self-proclaimed control freak, the experts couldn't understand how he ever agreed to such a deal. In response,

Redstone replies, "That didn't bother me because I always visualized that we would operate the company pretty much together" (Leonard, 2001).

Karmazin did not see the management of the organization in quite the same manner. In fact, he made this clear when he stated, "You have to have one person running the business. We decided when we did the merger that that person would be me" (Leonard, 2001).

Whether this was clear to both men at the time of the merger is not fully understood. Yet it was obvious to most people who knew the two that they would inevitably clash over certain aspects of the business.

Once the Viacom-CBS deal was announced, it did not take Karmazin long to assert his power and influence within the combined company. Moreover, he held nothing back. He made it public that he wanted 20% growth in every division, even the unpredictable movie business. His management style was very autocratic in nature. He wanted to be involved in everything and challenged Viacom's division heads relentlessly about how they operated their respective divisions. It was even rumored that he considered removing the free soda machines throughout the company and canceling employee bonuses (Leonard, 2001).

After some time on the job, however, Karmazin lightened up to a degree. The CBS and Viacom employees slowly got to know one another and were able to effectively and efficiently work together. Their combined efforts were able to significantly increase CBS ratings.

Redstone's New Role

For the most part, Redstone left Karmazin in charge. Per the agreement, he did not interfere with the daily activities of the business. On the surface, it appeared as though the two men had reached an appropriate working relationship. As one employee noted, "Sumner and Mel have worked out a terrific relationship. Sumner clearly is involved with the stock, investments, overseeing things. Mel is the operations guy" (Leonard, 2001).

However, others close to the situation were not buying into that claim. When a representative from *Fortune* magazine asked about the two leaders' schedules, a spokesperson said that they might not appear together in public for several months. When questioned why the two didn't appear together more frequently, Redstone replied:

> That's a good question. I never thought about it. I guess we're
> both so busy. While Mel legitimately has charge of day-to-day

operations, I'm in touch with all of our executives on a daily basis. Mel has encouraged everybody to stay in continual contact with me. I don't feel divorced from the operations. (Leonard, 2001)

Is his normal controlling manner, Sumner does concede that part of the reason he agreed to the merger is that Karmazin's contract is good for only three years. When it expires (December 2003), he can reorganize everything and be back in total control.

"I'm not saying it's going to happen. Mel is doing a terrific job. But, yeah, it's my call" (Redstone, as cited in Leonard, 2001).

In an evasive fashion, Mr. Redstone has refused to commit to renew Mr. Karmazin's existing contract when it expires. Additionally, Mr. Karmazin has made it clear that he will not accept any dilution of his operating control.

Ousting Karmazin would not be a simple task. First, 14 of 18 board votes are required. Eight of the board members originated from CBS and are considered loyal to Mr. Karmazin. Second, Wall Street has become very fond of Karmazin due to his efforts to increase earnings at CBS. According to one analyst, "If Mel leaves, the shares will take a hit. So Redstone, with $10 billion tied up in Viacom stock, might not want to shake this tree too hard" (as cited in Kadlec, 2002).

In an unsuccessful attempt to clear the air and ease the tension, a statement was issued by Viacom that said, "Neither Mr. Redstone nor Mr. Karmazin have stated their intentions beyond the end of the contract" (Peers, Flint, and Lippman, 2002).

The Epitome of Success

Sumner Redstone is Chairman of the Board and Chief Executive Officer of Viacom Inc. Under his guidance and leadership, the company has evolved into one of the largest entertainment and media companies in the world. In addition, the company is a leader in the production, promotion, and distribution of various forms of entertainment—including news, sports, and music.

As of this date, Viacom's properties include the CBS Network, MTV Networks, BET, Showtime Networks, Infinity Broadcasting, TDI Worldwide and Infinity Outdoor, Paramount Pictures, Paramount Television, Paramount Parks, UPN, Blockbuster, Simon & Schuster, and theatrical exhibition operations in North America and abroad.

The company's Internet businesses include the MTVi Group, the CBS Internet Group, and Nickelodeon Online. Additionally, Viacom owns half-interest in the Comedy Central cable channel. National Amusement, Inc., a closely held corporation that operates approximately 1,300 motion picture screens in the U.S., the U.K., and South America, is the parent company of Viacom (Viacom, 2002).

At an age when most people have been retired for 20 years…and with a wealth that most people couldn't even envision…Sumner Redstone keeps working as hard as ever. He works days, nights and weekends, and often exhausts much younger members of his staff.

> *"Viacom is me. I'm Viacom.*
> *That marriage is eternal, forever."* —Sumner Redstone

A Passion to Win

In an interview with *Executive Excellence* (2001), Redstone discussed a book that he and Peter Knobler authored…*A Passion to Win* (2001). His obsession to excel as well as his leadership philosophies are reflected in the following excerpts:

Question: Why the title, *A Passion to Win*?

Redstone: I've always wanted to win. I think winning is everything. Throughout my life I've had an obsessive drive to be number one. That doesn't mean I've always been number one. But that's what drives me…a desire to be the best at what I do.

Question: How do you keep that passion strong?

Redstone: You have to love what you do. I have a passion for Viacom…a true passion. Viacom is me, and I am Viacom. I don't mean that arrogantly. I simply mean that it's my life. I try to inspire a tremendous management team with the same sense of passion. If you really want to succeed, you have to be passionate. I have a will to win, and a commitment to excellence in performance. If you have both of those, and some intellectual capacity, nothing is impossible.

Question: What are the keys to managing talent?

Redstone: My secret is having a great management team. The way you manage talent is to let them run their business. If you have confidence in their talent, you do not intrude every time they make a decision. In major decisions and events, of course, I have discussions with them, but they decide what programs to run and what pictures to make. They may call me, but I made it clear to them that they are running the show.

Question: What do you look for in a manager?

Redstone: I look first for character and loyalty. I look for someone I can trust, and who trusts me. And, I look for confidence, competence, and commitment. These are all very important, but it's still sometimes not enough to succeed. Every manager will experience some failure.

Question: How do you deal with failure?

Redstone: I often say that success is not built on success, but rather on failure, frustration, and sometimes calamity.

Question: How do you stay optimistic when you experience setbacks?

Redstone: Optimism is not optional in business…it's vital. I believe that optimism is the only philosophy of life that's compatible with sustained success and sanity. So if you want to stay sane, you have to be optimistic. And part of optimism is having confidence in yourself. Now, as you have more success, your self-confidence increases. If you don't have confidence or don't trust yourself, you don't have a chance of winning.

Question: How do you create and maintain a culture of innovation and creativity?

Redstone: I think we've been able to maintain a high degree of innovation and creativity because we also have a high degree of financial discipline…and one works right alongside the other. We also cultivate creative talent…we attract a lot of creative young people who want to work in our industry. We train these people, and they become very good at what they do.

Question: How do you bring along creative talent?

Redstone: In each division, we train our people to understand that life in Viacom is a life of creativity…and then we export that creativity worldwide. I can safely say that what Viacom is doing globally in entertainment has never been done before. It's part of the creative drive of our culture; in a way, it thrives on itself.

Question: You say in your book that you're not saints but you do have a social conscience. What is the mission behind the money?

Redstone: Well, in the first place, money was never the driver. Most successful people are not motivated by money but by the desire to achieve, to win, to be the best. Sure money is important because we have to satisfy our stockholders. But I believe that social responsibility and the bottom line are compatible. There are times when any good company like Viacom has to say, "In this case, it's not about the bottom line...we have a social responsibility."

Question: Why keep seeking deals, debate, and honest feedback, when you could be surrounded by "yes men"?

Redstone: Who in their right mind would want to be surrounded by "yes men"? That's the last thing I want. I respect the views of the people around me. If they were morons, I wouldn't want their feedback. But I'm surrounded by brilliant people, many of whom could run Viacom. I respect their views, and I want to hear them. If they disagree with me, I want to hear that too. I want them to have some solid reasoning behind their position or point of view. But I respect and trust my team. One reason I know I can trust them is they know they can trust me. Mutual trust is the most important element in running a company. Without it, you lose. You don't last long. Where trust is lacking, there is not stability or loyalty. In contrast, we have a very stable management team...and that's important to all our stakeholders.

On a side note, Mr. Redstone agreed to donate the royalties earned from his book to Massachusetts General Hospital, where he spent months recovering after the 1979 hotel fire he survived. He also did not take an advance for the book (Cohen, 2001).

What Does the Future Hold?

> *"We all have to die someday. But I see no reason to*
> *hasten the process. I like what I'm doing*
> *and I want to stay around as long as I can."* —Sumner Redstone

In his above-referenced book, Sumner Redstone devotes some time and effort to describing his future. These remarks are interesting both from a psychological insight, and from a leadership insight.

So, what will I be doing five years from now? That is not a question I concern myself with. Nor am I particularly concerned about my age, although a great many others appear to be. If I am not yet ready to talk about succession, I am always very ready to talk about success. My enthusiasm for my job will not recede. The will to win is the will to survive, and I continue to have a passion to win. In that way I will always feel young.

Chronological age has little to do with intellectual capacity, the ability to work, the ability to lead. In fact, I often surprise my younger colleagues by being the first to accept and, indeed, suggest, new ideas and new agendas when the assumption is that I will hold on to the old ones like a bulldog.

What am I going to be doing five years from now? My industry is changing with the speed of light and I can say only that I want to continue in its brilliance. Now my concern is about what I will be doing tomorrow, next week, next month. There is work to be done and I am determined to do it the best way it can be done. I still want to be number one. (Redstone & Knobler, 2001, pp. 314-315)

References

Anonymous. (2001, September). A passion to win. *Executive Excellence*, 18, 9. Retrieved February 25, 2002, from ProQuest Direct database on the World Wide Web: http://proquest.umi.com

Cohen, L. (2001, April 5). Simon & Schuster is more than excited about a new author—and why not? *Wall Street Journal* [eastern edition], p. A.1. Retrieved March 2, 2002, from ProQuest Direct database on the World Wide Web: http://proquest.umi.com

Current Biography Yearbook. (1996). New York: The H.W. Wilson Co.

Kadlec, D. (2002, February 11). When two's a crowd: Does Viacom's founder have a problem letting go? Or is the heir apparent just too aggressive?. *Time*, 159, 6. Retrieved February 25, 2002, from Infotrac Direct database on the World Wide Web: web5.infotrac.galegroup.com.

Leonard, D. (2001, April 16). Who's the boss? *Fortune*, 143, 8. Retrieved February 19, 2002, from ProQuest Direct database on the World Wide Web: http://proquest.umi.com

Matzer, M. & Lenzner, R. (1994, October 17). Winning is the only thing. *Forbes*, 154, 9. Retrieved February 25, 2002, from Infotrac Direct database on the World Wide Web: web5.infotrac.galegroup.com.

Norris, F. (1999, September 8). The new improved Redstone still knows how to get his way. *New York Times* [late edition], p. 1. Retrieved March 2, 2002, from ProQuest Direct database on the World Wide Web: http://proquest.umi.com

Peers, M., Flint, J., & Lippman, J. (2002, February 4). Stability of power trio is critical to Viacom's future...*Wall Street Journal* [eastern ed], p. B.1. Retrieved February 25, 2002, from ProQuest Direct database on the World Wide Web: http://proquest.umi.com

Redstone, S. & Knobler, P. (2001). *A passion to win.* New York: Simon & Schuster.

Viacom (2002). *Sumner M. Redstone (The facts).* Retrieved February 25, 2002, from the World Wide Web: http://www.viacom.com/thefacts

Wasserstein, B. (1998). *The battle of control of America's leading corporations big deal.* New York: Warner Books, Inc.

Martha Stewart

Chairman and Chief Executive Officer
Martha Stewart Living Omnimedia

The CEO...at Home and at Work

In today's business environment, CEO's are generally portrayed as hard-driving tyrants at work, yet some are considered meek-mannered and timid once they enter the confines of their homes. The implication seems to be that chief executives often have a split personality...that they may be in control at work, but they may not be in control at home.

Because most Chief Executives strive to keep their home lives private, and because most executive spouses are well trained in the politics of letting their powerful mate take the lead in public, it's usually quite difficult to tell if there is any truth to the stereotype of the CEO's split personality.

Martha Stewart is a notable exception. Because she is a media star as well as a Chief Executive Officer, her every move is chronicled in the press. Her television persona as "The Perfect Homemaker" has made millions of people want to read about her life...both as a successful executive as well as a wife and mother. Due to her fame and fortune, several relatives, friends and ex-business associates have written about her in explicit detail.

The picture of Martha Stewart that emerges from all of this publicity may not be pretty...but it is remarkably consistent. It seems that Mrs. Stewart is the same person at home and at work. Her television persona aside, it seems that she is an extremely driven, demanding, difficult, demonstrative and detail-oriented person.

Chronology of Events...the Edited Version

Martha Stewart was born on August 3, 1941, in Jersey City, New Jersey. She was raised in a large, middle-class family; there were six children in total. During her youth, Martha lived a relatively modest yet comfortable life. Her parents, Martha and Eddie Kostyra, taught her the value of a strong work ethic at a very young age. The Kostyras instilled in their children some of the very values that their parents had taught them. One of the most important lessons conveyed to the children was that success comes through effort and hard work (Wooten, 1999).

With a family of eight, Martha's mother spent a good portion of her daily routine in the kitchen. Little did Martha know at the time that this would ultimately contribute to her later fame and fortune. Martha's father taught her his passion: gardening. Again, these were teachings that Martha would carry with her throughout her lifetime.

As a child, Martha spent the majority of her summers with her grandparents near Buffalo, New York. She would pick vegetables and fruit daily with her grandmother. It was then that she learned the art of preserving in glass jars.

Throughout her high school years, Martha was very studious; and, as a result, she earned stellar grades. According to Wooten (1999), she was determined to obtain a college degree, yet she knew she would have to fund her own education. At the young age of seventeen, she was able to secure a part-time modeling position at a local agency. Working at the modeling agency along with completing her daily household chores, Martha was still able to graduate in the top ten of her high school class. She was awarded a Rotary Club scholarship as a reward for high grades and exceptional leadership. She soon learned that she was accepted to Barnard College, located in New York City.

College was exciting and brought many changes for Martha. While she was a student at Barnard, she maintained her modeling career. She was featured in numerous magazines in the United States and France. This helped defray her educational expenses. She soon met Andy Stewart, a Yale Law School student. They became engaged in March 1961 and married in July 1961. Martha continued to model and Andy eventually took a position with a New York law firm. Their daughter, Alexis Gilbert, was born in September 1965. Martha was 24 years old when Alexis was born. Although considered a young mother, she was not considered a young model. She decided it was time to consider other career options; she subsequently landed a job as a stockbroker. Within two years, she was one of the top salespeople. It was in this position that she was able to witness how a business operates…experience that she capitalized on in later years (Wooten, 1999).

In 1972, the Stewarts purchased a country house in Westport, Connecticut…a wealthy community composed of many doctors, lawyers, and prominent business people. As they had done with previous homes, the Stewarts restored the house themselves to its original style. In time, Martha became increasingly bored with her job as a stockbroker. She resigned from her position and worked full-time on the final phases of her home restoration.

One day, while cooking in her kitchen, Martha decided she might want to pursue a career in the catering business. She put an advertisement in a local paper and received her first assignment: a 300-person wedding party. Her spectacular country kitchen became her headquarters. Her new endeavor turned into a huge success! The catering business took off like a bolt of lightning. She eventually gained national attention and appeared in popular magazines such as *Mademoiselle, House Beautiful,* and *Bon Appetit* (Wooten, 1999).

Martha's writing career started in 1980. Her first book, *Entertaining* (1982), was actually written by Liz Hawes, a long-time friend and freelance writer. The writer incorporated all of Martha's ideas on how to throw the ultimate elegant party. The book eventually became a bestseller, with 270,000 copies being sold after just three years. The publication of this book led to the development of numerous others. She soon became known as the authority on lifestyle.

Kmart Corporation

By 1986, nearly one million copies of Martha Stewart's first four books had been sold. During this time, Kmart was trying to acquire the perfect talent to promote its Home Products department. Martha Stewart fit the mold. This led to the deal that helped Kmart achieve organizational goals and promote Martha Stewart's interests as well. Stewart's line of home products were featured in Kmart stores throughout the United States. She agreed to appear in Kmart advertisements. In return, she would earn a very handsome salary in addition to the profits from the sale of her merchandise (Wooten, 1999).

Along with success, however, comes failure. In 1987, after 29 years of marriage, the Stewarts decided to separate. In 1990, the divorce was final. The split was far from amicable.

After the divorce was final, Martha bought another historic home that was built in 1838. She decided to tackle the renovation project on her own. Martha supervised and played an active role in the renovation process. She convinced interior decorators to decorate every room free of charge. It would be a showcase home, and people would pay to see the design ideas of professionals. The entire renovation process was captured in her tenth book, *Martha Stewart's New Old House* (1992).

Martha then decided to focus her efforts on a life-long dream...to develop a magazine of her own that would parallel her line of lifestyle books. Martha persuaded Time Warner to publish the magazine. On November 12, 1990, the upscale magazine appeared at newsstands. As with everything Martha touched, *Martha Stewart Living* was another tremendous success. In 1995, it was named by *Adweek* magazine as one of the "Ten Hottest Magazines of 1995"; in 1996, *Advertising Age* named the publication "Magazine of the Year." Time Warner agreed to a 10-year contract (Wooten, 1999).

Wooten (1999) explained Time Warner's initiative of an advertising campaign for Martha on NBC's *Today* show. Her acclaimed fame led Time Warner to believe that she would be just as successful in a weekly television show. Beginning in the fall of 1993, the *Martha Stewart* show was televised once a week for 30 minutes on the *Lifetime* network. Eventually the program grew to over 150 cable channels.

The Empire

The magazine, television show, and numerous books made Martha Stewart a true celebrity. Given her dominating personality, she soon realized that she desired complete control over everything that she created. She wanted the liberty to move her creation into any direction she desired.

In February 1997, Martha bought control of her magazine and all of her related businesses from Time Warner. She became the sole owner of her new company...Martha Stewart Living Omnimedia. The name was selected to encompass as many different media as possible. Martha Stewart holds the title of Chairman and Chief Executive Officer (Wooten, 1999).

Martha Stewart Omnimedia Profile

As depicted on the Martha Stewart Living Homepage (marthastewart.com), the company has two primary strategic objectives:

- To provide our original "how to" content and information to as many consumers as possible.

- To turn our consumers into "doers" by offering them the information and products they need for do-it-yourself ingenuity the "Martha Stewart way."

The company satisfies the first objective by distributing "how to" content throughout a myriad of media outlets. The compilation of these outlets has been dubbed as the "Omnimedia" platform. This platform includes the following:

- Three magazines, *Martha Stewart Living* (R), *Martha Stewart Weddings* (TM), and *Martha Stewart Baby*, along with periodic special interest magazines.

- The Emmy Award-winning and number-one-rated "how to" domestic arts television program in the Unites States, airing six episodes per week, plus a weekly segment on CBS This Morning.

- *From Martha's Kitchen* (TM), a daily cable television program.

- 34 books, which together have sold more than 10 million copies.

- A weekly *askMartha* (R) newspaper column, syndicated in over 230 newspapers.

- The *askMartha* radio program, airing on over 330 stations throughout the United States.

- The marthastewart.com website, with over 1.7 million registered users.

The second objective is accomplished through the creation of the unique "omnimerchandising" platform. This particular platform consists of more than 5,000 products, including bed and bath products, baby items, interior paints, craft kits, outdoor furniture garden tools, and housewares line. Consumers are provided with quality, convenience, and choice.

Merchandise is distributed through the following channels:

- The mass market discount channel in the United States and Canada.

- The national department store channel in the United States and Canada.

- Specialty paint stores and specialty craft and fabric stores across the United States.

- The *Martha by Mail* (R) upscale catalog.

- The online *Martha by Mail* store located at marthastewart.com.

- The shared Kmart website BlueLight.com.

These two platforms support four business segments: Publishing, Television, Merchandising, and Internet/Direct Commerce. The Internet/Direct Commerce business assists in satisfying both of the stated strategic objectives.

Awards and Honors

As noted on marthastewart.com, Stewart has been the recipient of many awards and honors. The following are a sampling of these achievements:

- *Vanity Fair* magazine selected Martha Stewart as number 42 in its annual New Establishment list of the top 50 leaders of the Information Age (October 2000).

- Named number 274 on *Forbes* magazine's annual "Forbes 400" list (October 2000).

- Named one of the "50 Most Powerful Women" by *Fortune* Magazine (October 1998 and October 1999).

- *Time* Magazine includes her in "America's 25 Most Influential People" (June 1996).

- Named "New York's 100 Most Influential Women in Business" in Crain's *New York Business* (June 1996).

- Earned six Daytime Emmy Awards: "Outstanding Directing in a Service Show" for the 1997-98 broadcast season; "Outstanding Service Show Host" in both the 1994-95 and 1996-97 broadcast seasons; and "Outstanding Services Show" in the 1994-95, 1998-99, and 1999-2000 broadcast seasons.

- The show has received a total of 29 Emmy nominations since its debut. In May 1998, Martha Stewart Living Television received the 1998 James Beard Foundation Award for the Best National Cooking Segment.

- Martha Stewart earned an Edison Achievement Award from the American Marketing Association (March 1998).

- Presented the HFN 1998 CEO Summit Award and was inducted into the National Sales & Marketing Hall of Fame (Fall 1998); HFN also named her the top lifestyle/designer for her Everyday products (September 1999).

- Selected as "Publishing Executive of the Year" by *Adweek* (March 1996).

- The recipient of a 1996 Matrix Award in the magazine category, honoring her as an outstanding woman in the communications industry (1996).

- Serves on the board of directors of the Magazine Publishers Association (MPA).

Martha Stewart in Action...the Unauthorized Version

Given Martha Stewart's awards, honors, and wealth, one would consider her to be the epitome of success. However, several unauthorized biographies of Stewart do not paint quite the happy, loving woman on television, radio, and print throughout the United States. Oppenheimer (1997) portrays Stewart as a business tyrant. He describes a micro-manager who watches the moves of her entire staff. She is obsessed with her career and expects her employees to be the same. In her early catering days, she would belittle her employees and reduce them to tears.

Stewart employed Marinda Freeman as executive director of Martha Stewart, Inc. According to Oppenheimer (1997), Freeman initially almost idolized Stewart, stating she was one who could relate to Stewart. As time progressed, however, a new twist surfaced.

Within the first six months after I started working there, Martha would begin writing me these two- and three- page single-spaced typed letters. They were raving, belittling, saying just awful, nasty, off-the-wall things about me personally. The letters contained wicked attacks, some of which involved criticism of my job, but most of which were on a personal level and had nothing to do with my professionalism. I would be reduced to tears.

Her *modus operandi* was always to attack after the fact, never to inform before. I never knew if I was supposed to be doing something or not doing something. It was only after the fact that she'd write these letters and say I was 'stupid' and 'a jerk.' I thought, 'Excuse me? Where did this come from? Business is booming right along, and then it's like this wham-o from outer space. It was like a Jekyll and Hyde thing.' (Oppenheimer, 1997, pp. 238-239)

Freeman experienced this emotional roller coaster for almost two years. She would eventually get the boot from Stewart. True to her nature, Stewart conducted the firing illogically. Freeman was on the telephone booking a flight for Martha:

All of a sudden Martha picked up the extension and started screaming into the phone at me at the top of her lungs, saying that I wasn't handling her reservations correctly. The woman on the other end must have thought we were all nuts. So I just hung up the phone, stood up, turned to Martha, who looked like a madwoman, a crazy person, a woman who was not rational, and said, 'I am not going to put up with your behavior anymore,' and I walked out the door. (Oppenheimer, 1997, p. 239)

Freeman applied for unemployment compensation only to be further harassed by Stewart. Martha attempted to block her from receiving any benefits. This forced Freeman to retain a lawyer. Freeman eventually won the case, as Stewart never appeared in court for the final hearing.

Some critics argue that this dual-personality of Martha Stewart stemmed from her bitter divorce from her husband, Andy Stewart. Although Andy thought a divorce could be finalized in six months, Martha had other plans. What was believed to take six months went on for years. Martha was fixated with getting everything she possibly could from her husband. Oppenheimer notes that "Martha's position was that since Andy had left the house, everything belonged to her" (1997, p. 282).

By the time Andy actually filed for divorce, he had fallen in love with Robyn Whitney Fairclough, who was 20 years younger than he. Fairclough was actually employed by Stewart in the mid-eighties. While the Stewarts were away, Fairclough would often house-sit, take care of the many pets, and run errands. Once Martha found out that Andy and Robyn were together, she refused to pay her for her services. Fairclough was forced to sue Martha in small claims court in 1988. Martha eventually paid her a portion of the money due her (Oppenheimer, 1997).

The divorce raged on for years. Martha convinced their daughter Alexis that her father abandoned her. To make matters worse, she bought Alexis whatever she wanted. She provided the best clothes and furnishings that money could buy. Martha clearly was trying to "buy" her daughter's love; she treated her as a girlfriend rather than a mother. Subsequently, Alexis did side with her mother and chose not to speak with her father. This was a heartbreaking experience for Andy.

While Andy and Martha were married, Andy was diagnosed with cancer. After the divorce, and Andy's later marriage to Robyn, Martha agreed to an interview with *McCall's* magazine. She said:

> The only regret I have in my entire life is that I don't have more children. That is a very serious regret. My husband had cancer that precluded him from having more children. And I didn't want to adopt. It was stupid. I'd give anything to have a son right now. (Oppenheimer, 1997, p. 359)

Andy responded to these false claims with a letter to the editor of *McCall's* magazine. He vehemently denied Martha's claim that he could not have children due to his medical condition. He proclaimed:

> The honest reason why Martha Stewart and I did not have more children is that our marriage was strained and painful and it provided an unhealthy atmosphere in which to bring up children. Our careers dominated, and we devoted far too little time to the child we had. We would have been even greater failures as parents if there had been a second child. Martha made it very clear at the time in many conversations between us and in conversations with friends that she did not want another child...to put a more sympathetic spin on her personal story at my expense, she untruthfully offered my cancer as the reason. (Oppenheimer, 1997, p. 360)

Allegations of Andy's cancer preventing him to have children proved to be false. On March 19, 1997, two months after Martha retracted her story, Robyn Fairclough Stewart gave birth to two beautiful, healthy twin girls. Additionally, they had previously adopted an infant boy.

Martha's staff members never knew which personality would prevail each and every day. One of her editors noted:

> She'd change from being the sweetheart. I once dropped a piece of ice cream on the kitchen floor while we were shooting, and she just blew up. I'd been doing this kind of work for thirty-five years, so I just knew to walk very, very gently, be careful. If I said the wrong thing, did the wrong thing, belched at the wrong time, I'd be in trouble. She would have these blowouts with Andy, and it would show on her face, and then somebody who was in her inner circle—her mother, or her sister Laura, or whoever—would come out to the set and say, 'Watch out, Martha's in really terrible shape today.' But my God, she'd get on the set, the lights would go on, and she'd be Martha Stewart, no matter what. (Oppenheimer, 1997, p. 300)

Another employee revealed, "She was sour. She was unpleasant. She was angry. It was horrible. Martha was a nightmare" (p. 300). Still another employee classified Stewart as a perfectionist.

> It was difficult to do things the way she wanted. I was taking things from her house to decorate the set, and she was obviously concerned about getting them back in the right place. She even suggested I take Polaroid pictures before I removed something, so I'd know where to put it back. Her life was so regimentally scheduled that she didn't really have time for a lot of niceties. She was intimidating, very demanding, and could be really bitchy. Occasionally I had to put on her clothes for these hand shoots, and she was perfectly rude. She'd say, 'this is a seven-hundred-dollar Donna Karan alligator belt, just so you know.' I had never known her before as a celebrity, and she would vacillate between feeling entitled to a lot of attention and being insecure. (pp. 304-305)

Martha's apparent obnoxious leadership style was not only limited to her business affairs. Brother Frank Kostyra once approached her with an entrepreneurial idea. The idea was to design and produce a line of Martha Stewart logo aprons to be sold exclusively through the Kmart retail chain. The aprons would complement the already existing Martha Stewart line found in the stores. Frank spent his own time and money in an attempt to make sure the concept was viable. After a laborious process, Frank determined that his idea was a sure success. He crunched the numbers and approached Martha with his thought:

> I laid it at her feet and told her that Laura could be involved, that Mom could get involved, that it would help the whole family, and that we would all come away filthy rich.

> But Martha wouldn't bite. 'No one in this family is going to come riding in on *my* coattails,' she snarled. 'You're not coming in on *my* success.' When he described his sister's response to their mother, she shrugged knowingly. 'Well, Frank, you know how she is: Martha's Martha.' (Oppenheimer, 1997, p. 305)

Enraged with anger over his sister's reaction, Frank decided to go public with the "true" Martha Stewart. In 1996, he sold tell-all stories to various tabloids.

Martha's sister, Laura Hebert, was employed by Martha. While in Miami shooting a Kmart spot, Martha blew up at her sister. Patricia Hirsch was one of the creative directors on site. According to Hirsch (as cited in Oppenheimer, 1997, p. 309), the following episode took place:

> A bunch of us were having dinner at Joe's Pier, and we all were having a drink before dinner. When Laura ordered a second drink, Martha snapped at her sister and said something really nasty, and Laura just broke down sobbing. It was an embarrassing situation. Martha certainly was mean to her. It was terrible. Laura was working for Martha, and Martha laid a lot on her sister and put her through pure hell, bossing her around, treating her like the maid, always being very sharp with her. For Martha to do that to her own sister in front of people from a production company, an advertising agency, and the client was a little nuts.

Her relationship with Kmart Corporation and eventually Time Warner was nothing less than rocky at times. The relationship almost bordered on blackmail. Kmart, for example, had many reservations about Martha's unpredictable behavior. Yet, she was golden for the organization; sales of the Martha Stewart line enhanced the bottom line for Kmart. An executive at Kmart corporation noted the following:

> Martha doesn't pay for anything, and she would bleed a stone if it was possible. She wanted to get whatever she could get out of Kmart. Martha abused almost everything. If she came into head-

quarters for a day and a half, her personal telephone bill would be two hundred dollars...Martha wouldn't do anything for free. When I was involved with her, I didn't know of a charity event that she ever did for free. When she traveled, she'd have cars pick her up. She'd reserve the best hotel suites. She flew first class. (Oppenheimer, 1997, p. 307)

She went on to say:

When the woman who was in charge of checking Martha's expense account questioned her charges, Martha would rip her from one end to the other. (p. 307)

Her rapport with Time Warner was not on the best of terms either. In January 1997, after laborious negotiations, Martha agree to pay approximately $75 million for control of her magazine and subsidiary operations. In the end, Time Warner was pleased to cut the ties with Martha Stewart. However, one Time Warner conceded, "We didn't want out, Martha wanted out. She wanted to be in control of her own destiny" (Oppenheimer, 1997, p. 359).

The Martha Stewart Legacy

It would appear that Martha Stewart has paid a high price for her fame and fortune...at least in terms of strained and broken relationships with friends, relatives and business partners. Many of the people who dislike Martha Stewart secretly rejoiced upon learning that she was under investigation of Federal Obstruction of Justice charges regarding her sale of nearly 4,000 shares of ImClone stock. It was alleged that Stewart was part of an insider trading scandal masterminded by ImClone CEO Samuel Waksal just prior to the public announcement that his company's highly-touted cancer drug, Erbitux, had been rejected by the Food and Drug Administration.

While there are many successful female Chief Executive Officers that would exemplify success, Martha Stewart merits a part in a leadership book for two very important reasons. One, her status as a media personality as well as a Chief Executive Officer enables others to examine her leadership style in great detail...based on authoritative writings of relatives, friends and employees. Two, her management style exemplifies the now outdated system of managing by means of fear and intimidation. This management style was prevalent in the early decades of the 20th century, when it was almost universally believed that workers had to be "driven" rather than "led."

There is no disputing her success...and no disputing the fact that she has worked exceptionally hard to achieve that success. The "Perfect Home-maker" may not be the "Perfect Chief Executive Officer"; but her story is an interesting one...and her success is undeniable.

References

Martha Stewart Living Omnimedia. (n.d.). *Biography*. Retrieved August 14, 2001, from the World Wide Web: http://www.marthastewart.com/about_martha/bio/index.asp

Martha Stewart Living Omnimedia. (n.d.). *Company Overview*. Retrieved August 14, 2001, from the World Wide Web: http://www.marthastewart.com

Meachum, V. (1998). *Martha Stewart Successful Businesswoman*. Berkeley Heights, NJ: Enslow Publishers, Inc.

Oppenheimer, J. (1997). *Martha Stewart—Just Desserts*. New York: William Morrow & Company, Inc.

Wooten, S. (1999). *Martha Stewart America's Lifestyle Expert*. Woodbridge, CT: Blackbirch Press, Inc.

Donald J. Trump

Chairman and Chief Executive Officer
Trump Hotels and Casino Resorts

"As long as you're going to think anyway, think big." —Donald Trump

Donald Trump is one of, if not, the most recognizable and "entertaining" of all business leaders in America. It has been said that he could just as easily be on the cover of the *National Enquirer* as on the cover of *Forbes* or *Business Week*. He is known as America's quintessential dealmaker, the world's most famous developer, the modern Midas, the entrepreneur's entrepreneur and the P.T. Barnum of Finance.

From a Family of Entrepreneurs

Donald Trump comes from a family of entrepreneurs. His grandfather Frederick was originally a barber who came from the Pfalz region of Germany at the end of the 19th century to make his fortune in the far west and in the gold fields of Alaska. Frederick Trump had the insight to see that more money was to be made supporting the gold rush than on the front line with a pick and shovel. He opened a restaurant in Seattle and he then operated a saloon in the Klondike. After the gold rush, he moved to New York City. Sadly, Frederick died at a relatively young age (Blair). His son Fred was forced to step in to help make ends meet for the family.

Fred was originally a carpenter. However, he inherited the entrepreneur spirit from his father. This helped him to see moneymaking opportunities. After the Second World War, he was able to capitalize on the pent-up demand for family housing by going into the real estate business. His focus was on constructing and running middle income apartments in Queens, Staten Island and Brooklyn (Biography.com). When Fred died in 1999, he had assets worth between $200 and $300 million.

Early Life

Donald was born in the Queens borough of New York City in 1946 and was the fourth of five children. He grew up as an apprentice in his father's real estate business. He also learned about certain parts of the business that he did not especially like: collecting rent and physical labor. Fred was wealthy enough to send Donald to a private high school. He went to the New York Military Academy at 13. After graduation he attended Fordham University for two years. However, Fordham did not have the program that Donald really wanted: real estate. For this, he had to transfer to the Wharton School of Finance at the University of Pennsylvania. He graduated from the Wharton School in 1968.

Donald got a very good lesson in high stakes real estate through a venture with his father's Trump Organization while he was still in college. Fred Trump decided to buy a rundown apartment complex in Cincinnati that was in bankruptcy. Without having to invest any money of their own, Fred and Donald were able to get financing for the apartment complex through government-sponsored programs at an amount that was far above the purchase price of $6 million dollars. They used the additional funds to renovate the apartment complex. They were able to turn this failing operation around through aggressive rent collection and by improving its appearance. They were then able to sell the apartments at a substantial profit. This was an excellent proving ground for Donald's future multi-million dollar deals.

Donald Takes on Manhattan

After graduating from college, Donald moved to Manhattan to begin his own deal-making career. He moved into a less-than-upscale apartment, but by setting up residency in Manhattan he was better able to assess the property values and opportunities. Donald determined that he needed to acquire "connections" to succeed in the Manhattan real estate business. He determined that membership in an exclusive private club would serve as the vehicle to achieve his goal. Using his persuasive talents, he was able to convince the manager of *Le Club* to let him become a member. This membership was conditional, however. He was not to "hit" on any of the wives of the existing members. It is not known if he complied with the conditions, but he did use his membership in *Le Club* to make business contacts. *Le Club's* membership included CEOs, models and millionaires (Wilber).

In 1974, at age 28, he convinced the city to build a convention center on the grounds of the bankrupt Penn Central railroad yards. The Trump Organization was able to secure purchase options for two Penn Central waterfront sites at a cost of $62 million. He was able to accomplish this without any money down. In addition to making a bid to build the convention center, Trump offered to forego part of his fee if the complex was named after the Trump family. Both the bid to build the center and the name suggestion were rejected by the city. It would be named after Senator Jacob Javits (Biography.com). Later that year, he successfully negotiated with the city and the Hyatt Corporation to renovate the old Penn Central Commodore Hotel. In 1980, the project was completed and the renamed Grand Hyatt Hotel was open for business. This successful project helped to give Trump his celebrity status.

Trump's Decade: The 1980s

It was during the '80s that Donald Trump came to prominence nationally. This was the time that he gained the reputation as a real estate tycoon and the ultimate dealmaker. In 1982, he built the Trump Tower on Fifth Avenue for $200 million. This elaborate 58-story apartment and retail complex had a six story glass atrium with an 80-foot waterfall (Biography.com). After the Trump Tower, the next project was the Trump Plaza. This would be the tenth casino in Atlantic City. It had 614 rooms (including 85 luxury suites for high rollers), seven restaurants, a health club, and a showroom with a seating capacity for 740.

Trump committed $22 million to the project when Harrahs/Holiday Inns Inc. came into the picture. For half interest in the project, they reimbursed Trump the $22 million he had already invested. They also paid him an additional $50 million in cash plus financing in amounts estimated to be between $170 and $250 million. The total cost of the project was reported to be $220 million. That meant that Trump came away with a handsome profit plus 50 percent interest in the new hotel-casino without risking any of his own money! (Piccolo)

His next Atlantic City hotel-casino would be the Trump Castle. This was completed in 1985. The proposed name was the Trump Palace. However, Caesar's Palace in Las Vegas sued on the grounds that this was a name infringement. A third Atlantic City project, Taj Mahal, would be the largest hotel-casino in the world. There were other additions to the Trump organization. In 1983, he bought the New Jersey Generals football franchise of the United States Football League for six million dollars. By the end of the decade, the Trump empire would also include Trump Parc, the Trump Shuttle Airline, and 24,000 apartments. Trump's personal wealth was estimated to be $1.7 billion.

The Trump Business Model

You can initially trace Donald Trump's success to his solid understanding of the real estate business. He gained this knowledge through his father, his education at the Wharton School and through experience. He then specialized in real estate of the rich and famous. Because Mr. Trump knew the psychology of the wealthy, he raised his prices when the competition lowered theirs. Whether the higher prices were justified did not really matter. The steep price served to convey an image that his property was "first class."

Donald Trump's greatest asset is his ability to promote himself. He has been called the "P.T. Barnum of Finance." He has almost no public relations office to speak of. That's because he is the public relations. He answers most reporters' calls personally. This PR skill would open many doors for him. Trump demonstrated that if you portray yourself as a winner, banks and the government would fall over themselves to provide financial backing for high cost and high-risk projects. Donald Trump mastered the art of leveraging other people's money to build his empire.

Besides promoting himself, he also promotes all of his holdings using the Trump name. Almost everything that he owns has the word "Trump" in it. Besides apartment buildings, casinos and hotels, there is even a Trump golf course. He even licensed his name for a building in South Korea. For this, he received $5 million. By having his name plastered everywhere, this served to promote the individual "Donald Trump." This reinforcing promotion of both the individual and the empire has made Donald Trump one of, if not the, most recognizable of all the corporate leaders in America. His high profile lifestyle (business and personal) serves to keep him in the public eye. According to the Gallup organization, 98 percent of all Americans know who he is. The Trump Tower has become a major New York tourist attraction. To top off the (self and empire) promotion campaign, Donald Trump's 1987 book: *Trump: The Art of a Deal* was a Number 1 National Bestseller. In 1990, he had another bestseller: *Trump: Surviving at the Top.*

The following are Donald's "Trump Cards" from *The Art of a Deal.*

Think Big

Most people think small, because most people are afraid of success, afraid of making decisions, afraid of winning.

Protect the Downside and the Upside Will Take Care of Itself

If you plan for the worst—if you can live with the worst—the good will always take care of itself.

Maximize Your Options

I keep a lot of balls in the air, because most deals fall out no matter how promising they seem at first.

Know Your Market

...I don't hire a lot of number-crunchers, and I don't trust fancy market surveys. I do my own surveys and draw my own conclusions. I ask and I ask and I ask, until I begin to get a gut feeling about something. And that's when I make a decision.

Use Your Leverage

The best thing you can do is deal from strength, and leverage is the biggest strength you can have. Leverage is having something the other guy wants. Or better yet needs. Or best of all, simply can't do without.

My leverage came from confirming an impression they were already predisposed to believe.

Enhance Your Location

Perhaps the most misunderstood concept in all real estate is that the key to success is location, location, location. Usually, that's said by people who do not know what they are talking about.

What you need is the best deal. Just as you can create leverage, you can enhance a location, through promotion and through psychology.

Get the Word Out

You can have the most wonderful product in the world, but if people don't know about it, it's not going to be worth much. You need to generate interest, and you need to create excitement.

Fight Back

[W]hen people treat me badly or unfairly or try to take advantage of me, my general attitude all my life has been to fight back very hard.

Deliver the Goods

You can't con people, at least not for long. You can create excitement, you can do wonderful excitement, you can do wonderful promotion and get all kinds of press, and you can throw in a little hyperbole. But if you can't deliver the goods people will eventually catch on.

Contain the Costs

I believe in spending what you have to. But I also believe in not spending more than you should.

...you can dream great dreams, but they'll never amount to much if you can't turn them into reality at a reasonable cost.

Trump was successful in the eighties because he had diversified into a number of areas. As it turned out, about one in five of his major investments would have a major payback. This strategy works in good times (it also helps if you are truly diversified). Unfortunately, Trump's investments and his entire empire, for that matter, were highly skewed in just one market: real estate.

In the Dumps

The Trump Empire started to unravel in 1990. He was unable to make payments of over $2 billion that were due on bank loans. To avoid bankruptcy, he was able to secure emergency financing to restructure his debt. However, in the process he was forced to divest control of many of his most valuable holdings (Wilber). This included the Trump Shuttle, some of the casinos and the Plaza Hotel. *Forbes* estimates that the Trump empire's net worth went from $17 billion in 1989 to $500 million in 1990. Trump ran into trouble because he fell victim to the combined effects of a heavily leveraged operation and a downturn in the real estate business cycle. Trump got into this awkward position, in part, because he had so successfully promoted himself. "Banks that never lent money for gambling businesses before lined up to fund Trump's empire, more for his name, his golden touch and because of his earlier real estate deals." (Wilber)

The Comeback

During the nineties, Trump went from being almost a billion dollars in debt to having an estimated worth of over two billion dollars. This story was documented in Trump's third bestseller *Trump: the Art of a Comeback*.

In 1995, Trump took Trump Hotels & Casino Resorts (THCR) public. This stock offering raised $140 million, which was used to help pay his creditors. Trump owns forty percent of THCR. It now appears that Trump's glory days of the '80s are back. Trump began to rebuild his empire. In 1996, THCR acquired two hotel casinos: the Taj Mahal and Trump's Castle. He would later acquire Trump Plaza Hotel and Casino, the Trump Indiana Riverboat Casino, Warner Brothers Studio Store, the Empire State Building and the Hard Rock Café. He is also owns the rights to the Miss Teen USA, Miss USA, and Miss Universe beauty pageants. His empire employs 22,000.

Trump's gambling operations are doing very well. His three New Jersey casinos take in approximately a third of all the Atlantic City gaming revenues.

The Wit and Wisdom (and Arrogance) of Donald Trump

"I remember walking down Fifth Avenue in 1991 with Marla, and we saw a bum with a change cup selling pencils. Marla said, 'Isn't that terrible, that poor man.' ... And I said, 'Yes, it is terrible, but right now, he's worth $900 million more than me.'"

"Part of being a winner is knowing when enough is enough. Sometimes you have to give up the fight and walk away, and move on to something that's more productive."

"I try to learn from the past, but I plan for the future by focusing exclusively on the present. That's were the fun is."

"I aim very high, and then I just keep pushing to get what I am after."

"I'm the biggest developer in the hottest city in the world."

"Always have a pre-nup."

"In the end, you're measured not by how much you undertake, but by what you finally accomplish."

Family Life and Post Family Life

It is very hard to separate the public Donald Trump from the private Donald Trump. He has been a mainstay in the tabloids for over twenty years. Most of the stories focused on his stormy relationship with his two wives: Ivana Trump and Marla Maples. He married the very glamorous former model, Ivana Zelnickova Winklmayr, in 1977. Ivana had been an alternate on the Czech Olympic Ski team in 1968. Ivana would play an active role in Trump's organization; she was the Vice President in charge of design (Biography.com). Donald and Ivana had three children: Donald Jr. born in 1978, Ivanka in 1982, and Eric in 1986. The marriage to Ivana was on the rocks in 1990 as a result of Donald's highly publicized affair with Marla Maples. Donald and Ivana divorced in 1991. The settlement for Ivana included $10 million in cash, a $12 million home in Connecti-cut, $350,000 a year in alimony and $300,000 in child support (*Love, American Style!*, 1997).

Trump married Marla Maples in 1993 in an elaborate ceremony with

thousands in attendance at the Trump Plaza Hotel. They had a daughter, Tiffany, born two months before the marriage. Trump separated from Marla four years later. They finally divorced in 1999. The settlement was estimated to be in the $2.5 million range (*Love, American Style!*, 1997).
His current interest is Slovenian "supermodel" Melania Knauss.

Little Known (and Bizarre)

- Donald Trump had a $100 million yacht that had been owned by Adnan Khashoggi, a Saudi financier (*Man of the Week*).

- His favorite words are "plush," "No. 1," and "super luxury" (Berton).

- He does not like to delegate. Trump believes that if you want the job done right you do it yourself. He is known for closely supervising (and yelling) at construction projects. His obsession with detail leads him to personally negotiate with subcontractors himself rather than to leave this function to a purchasing department. He will do whatever it takes to close a deal. This includes calling a subcontractor's mother to wish her a happy birthday.

- In 1999, he considered running for President in Ross Perot's Reform Party. His campaign theme: What the country really needs is a successful businessman to run the country, not bureaucrats. He later downplayed his run for President by saying that he was too honest to be a politician.

- As a master showman, it should come as no surprise that he enjoys doing cameo appearances on both TV and in movies. He has played himself such TV shows as: *Roseanne, Suddenly Susan, Spin City, The Nanny, The Fresh Prince of Bel-Air,* and *The Job.* He has also been in the following movies: *Home Alone 2, Lost in New York, Celebrity, and 54* (Man of the Week).

- Reminiscent of the billionaire Howard Hughes, Trump has an aversion to microbes. He does not like to shake hands with anyone unless they are wealthy, powerful or attractive (Berton). In his third book *Comeback,* he says that he admires the way that the Japanese greet each other by bowing.

• There is an urban legend that Trump will neither confirm nor deny. According to the story, Trump's limo broke down on the Garden State Parkway. An unemployed auto mechanic offered his assistance. He was able to get the limo running again. However, the mechanic refused to accept any payment for his services. Trump was so impressed with this benevolent act that he sent flowers to the mechanic's wife with a certified letter saying that their mortgage had been paid in full (Gross).

Liked and Disliked

"He is the poster boy for Lifestyles of the Rich and Famous."

"...a man as likely to appear on the cover of Business Week as on National Enquirer."

"...according to the Gallup Organization, 98% of Americans know who he is." (*Man of the Week*)

"Donald Trump's cocky, devil-may-care business persona leaves few people neutral."

"People love him, people hate him, but either way, people love to watch him." David Russo, Executive Producer of the "Billionaire" (Wagner, 2001)

"He is a true American original, with great instincts and billion-dollar dreams." (*Reviews*)

"Donald Trump is an American icon, having combined as much money with as little taste as possible." (*Love, American Style!*, 1997)

"For Donald Trump and Martha Stewart, their enterprises are intentional personifications of their own public personas." (Anderson)

Here is what Donald Trump has to say to those critics who are so quick to dismiss him.

"Anyone who thinks my story is anywhere near over is sadly mistaken."

References

Anderson, J. (n.d.). *Persuasive leadership.* Retrieved August 21, 2002, from www.andersonleadership.com/ideas/persldrshp/persldrshp.html

Berton, P. (n.d.). *Trump: The art of the vulgarian.* Retrieved August 21, 2001, from www.canoe.ca/JamBooksReviewsA/artof_trump.html

Trump, Donald (John). (n.d.). *Biography.com.* Retrieved July 21, 2002, from http://search.biography.com/print_record.pl?id=20210

Blair, G. (n.d.). *The Trumps: Three generations that built an empire* [Review by Roger Gathamhe]. Retrieved August 21, 2002, from http://www.spencerstuart.com/execlife/content/en/us/readingroom-review.asp

Gross, R. (n.d.). www.casinocenter.com/journal/june/trump.htm

Love, American style! (1997, October 20). *The New York Daily News.* Retrieved August 21, 2002, from http://theoutrage.com/library/971020.html

Man of the Week: Donald Trump. (n.d.). Retrieved August 21, 2002, from http://www.askmen.com/men/business_politics/38_donald_trump.html

Piccolo, S. (n.d.). *Gaming in Atlantic City.* Retrieved August 21, 2002, from www.chequers.com/ACGaming/part7.htm

Reviews. (n.d.). Retrieved August 21, 2002, from http://hallbiographies.com/professionals_academics/92.shtml

Russo, D. (2001, February 19). *Casino News.* Retrieved August 21, 2002, from www.online-casino-gambling-guide.com/CasinoNews/200102_2292.htm

Trump, D. & Schwartz, T. (1987). *Trump: The art of a deal.* New York: Warner Books.

Trump, D. & Leerhseen, C. (1990). *Trump: Surviving at the top.* New York: Random House.

Trump, D. & Bohner, K. (1997). *Trump: The art of a comeback.* New York: Times Books.

Wagner, L. (2001, February 17). *Trump tries reality TV.* Retrieved August 21, 2002, from http:///xarda.com/donaldTrump.html

Wilber, M. (n.d.). *Donald Trump.* Retrieved August 21, 2002, from www.stfrancis.edu/ba/ghkickul/stuwebs/bbios/biograph/trump.htm

Ted Turner
Vice Chairman
Time Warner

An Abusive Beginning

Robert Edward "Ted" Turner was born to Ed and Florence Turner on November 19, 1938. The elder Turner was both a demanding husband and a demanding father. Only after marrying Ed, did Florence discover his dark characteristics: he was intolerant, deceptive, and manipulative. He was also an alcoholic, which eventually took a toll on the entire family.

Ed Turner was a taskmaster who believed that frequent beatings of his son would build his character. Often, he would deliver physical and verbal punishments that went well beyond what was considered normal parenting. According to some reports, he even beat Ted with a wire coat hanger (Current Biography Yearbook, 1998). Due to his father's beatings, one would think that Ted would become a passive, timid, fearful child. But, as time would tell, the future billionaire developed just the opposite characteristics.

In 1950, the Turners sent Ted off to a military academy, The McCallie School, in Chattanooga, Tennessee. Ted initially hated McCallie. He was

153

a prankster, he teased his teachers mercilessly, and he regularly received disciplinary punishment. This is where he first earned the nickname, "Terrible Ted." In his own words,

> I did everything I could to rebel against the system, although I think I believed in it from the beginning. I was always having animals in my room and stuff like that, and getting into trouble one way or another, and then having to take the punishment like a man. I wanted to be the best, and I saw that it could be done if you worked at it. (Fischer, 1993, p. 17)

During this same time period, Turner learned the devastating fate of his only sister, Mary Jane. She was diagnosed with severe lupus, a disease that left her susceptible to many other viruses. An encephalitis attack resulted in brain damage that caused her to experience fits for eight years before her actual death in 1958 (Fischer, 1993).

On a positive note, the school's military atmosphere seemed to agree with Turner. He earned the rank of Captain and received various honors and awards throughout his stay. He was also an active participant in the school's sailing program, and this is where his passion for boating was developed.

In 1960, Ted Turner married Judy Nye Hallisey. They had two children from this marriage...Laura Lee and Robert Edward IV. The marriage did not last long, however; and their divorce was finalized in the early 1960s. Turner not only had a passion, but an obsession, for winning. In fact, it was rumored that he once irately rammed his boat into his wife's boat when it looked like she might win a race in which the two of them were competing (Current Biography Yearbook, 1998).

Turner second marriage was to Jane Smith, an airline attendant. They were married in 1964, and they had two sons and a daughter...Beauregard, Rhett, and Jennie. This marriage lasted for 24 years, but the two eventually grew apart and divorced in 1988.

After a couple of years as one of America's most eligible bachelors, Turner began courting the actress and fitness guru Jane Fonda. They were married on December 21, 1991. This marriage, too, would result in divorce. Ted Turner was single again in the spring of 2001 (Schwed, 2002).

"I'll Do it My Way"

Ted Turner is probably as famous for his personal life as he is for his business ventures. In particular, he is very well known for his outspokenness and brash personality. "I'll do it my way" is a phrase that Ted Turner vehemently adheres to...and he has always done things his own way. This outspoken billionaire, champion yachtsman, and founder of Cable News Network and Turner Network is a daredevil risk taker. He is intellectually curious and willing to gamble...even though some of his gambles do not pay off.

Despite being nicknamed "The Mouth of the South" and "Captain Outrageous" for his biased opinions, Turner has developed a communications empire based on the foundation of his father's billboard business. While he is generally depicted as brash and domineering, he willingly shares his fortune with various environmental and charitable organizations that he feels are worthwhile.

Turner displayed his independence and creativity quite early in life. "Terrible Ted" developed some rather eccentric habits in his youth...habits such as practicing amateur taxidermy and growing lawn grass in his room. He was asked to leave Brown University after he was caught with a woman in his private quarters.

He was the winner of America's Cup in 1977 with his yacht *Courageous*...and then showed up drunk to collect the prize. He has been known to wear a Confederate officer's uniform, replete with sword, to corporate negotiations. He tried to manage the Atlanta Braves (a team that he owns) from the dugout during a particularly bad season. He even went so far as to challenge his rival media mogul, Rupert Murdoch, to a televised boxing match in Las Vegas (ABCNews.com, 2001).

WTCG: Turner Communications Group grows to Turner Broadcasting System (TBS)

Although it appears on the surface that Turner may have reached self-actualization on Maslow's hierarchy of needs, the inner Turner has faced some serious setbacks in his life. He has been treated for depression, and he was only 24 when his father Ed, despondent over financial difficulties, committed suicide with the fatal blow of a gun.

After his father's death, Ted took over at the helm of the family business. He decided to expand the company into the television business, purchasing a struggling Atlanta UHF station (Channel 17) in 1970. Through strategic programming acquisitions, Turner eventually made the station successful. The "new-and-improved" station was renamed WTCG, the last three letters being an acronym for "Turner Communications Group" (ABCNews.com, 2001).

After learning enough about the television industry to feel comfortable with it, Turner's next goal was to tackle the fledgling cable industry. He had discovered cable systems long ago, and finally decided that he, along with Home Box Office, would take the plunge and buy the necessary equipment required to broadcast via satellite. The venture was a gamble, but Turner always thrived on this sort of risk.

In December 1976, Channel 17 began beaming its signal via satellite to cable systems all around the nation...and Superstation TBS (Turner Broadcasting System) was born. By the end of 1978, Turner's station was reaching two million homes, more than double the number it had previously been capable of reaching (Current Biography Yearbook, 1998).

In 1979, the company changed its name to Turner Broadcasting System, Inc. (TBS, Inc.) and the call letters became WTBS. Using the profits from WTBS, which was then the flagship of his nationwide Turner Broadcasting System, Turner launched CNN. Despite many naysayers, the 24-hour all-news cable channel turned into gold with the coverage of such memorable events as the space shuttle *Challenger* disaster in 1986 and the Persian Gulf War in 1991.

Competition Strikes

"The only way they're going to rid of me is to put a bullet through me."
—Ted Turner

As with any successful venture, competition was forthcoming. In 1982, ABC and Westinghouse joined together and attempted to develop their own 24-hour cable news network. This Satellite News Channel (SNC) would offer an updated news report every half hour. This did not sit well with "Terrible Ted." In an effort to counter this attack, Turner launched Headline News, which also presented updated news reports every half hour.

> I figured, knowing they were two big companies and that they were both public corporations, and how slow those kinds of operations usually run, that if their losses were bigger than anticipated, the people in charge of this project would come under criticism...and I knew that if they ran into unanticipated diffi-

culties there would be friction between the two fifty-fifty partners.

You're much better off competing against a split command than against a single command because split commands spend a lot of time trying to figure out what to do and so it's easy for them to get into an argument. I find that partnerships work okay when things are going well, but they are put under a great deal of strain when things don't go as anticipated.

So even though we were very, very strapped financially, and they knew it, I decided that we would beat them to the market. We would split the market for that service, so they would not be as viable. I didn't know exactly how long we could last. I think the two of them had resources a hundred times greater than mine. I did know that in a war of attrition, we'd lose. (Brands, 1999, pp. 283-284)

In the long-run, it turned out that Ted Turner had once again made the right move. SNC's losses in the first year were too much for ABC and Westinghouse to stomach, and Turner eventually bought out the rival news network.

CNN did not actually turn a profit until 1985. Along the way, however, it had become a very valuable brand name. Due to its international coverage, CNN had become the news channel of choice for leaders around the world. George Bush, Sr. was even quoted as saying, "I learn more from CNN than I do from the CIA" (as cited in Current Biography Yearbook, 1998, p. 576).

Turner Broadcasting System, Inc.'s growth didn't end there, however. The system continued to grow rapidly, and added the following networks and businesses:

- TBS Superstation

- Turner Network Television (TNT)

- Cartoon Network

- Turner Classic Movies (TCM)

- Turner South

- Boomerang

- TNT Europe
- Cartoon Network Europe
- TNT Latin America
- Cartoon Network Latin America
- TNT & Cartoon Network/Asia Pacific
- Atlanta Braves
- Atlanta Hawks
- Atlanta Thrashers
- Goodwill Games
- Cartoon Network Japan
- Cable News Network (CNN)
- CNN Headline News
- CNN International
- CNNfn
- CNN/Sports Illustrated
- CNN en Espanol
- CNN Airport Network
- CNNRadio Noticias
- CNN Interactive, CNN Newsource
- CNN+
- CNN Turk (Turner Broadcasting System, 2001a)

Turner: The "Philanthropist"

"That list [Forbes magazine's list of the wealthiest Americans] is destroying our county! These new super-rich won't loosen up their wads because they're afraid they'll reduce their net worth and go down on the list. That's their Superbowl." —Ted Turner

In the mid-1980s, Turner focused on philanthropy. His Goodwill Games, originally held in Moscow in 1986, were both a publicity event for Turner Broadcasting and a genuinely intended contribution to world peace. The Turner Foundation, established in 1990, gives millions of dollars yearly to environmental causes. Additionally, in 1994, Turner donated $200 million to the cause. In 1997, his gift of $1 billion to a new foundation to support the United Nations may have been the largest single donation by a private individual in history (Hamilton, 1999).

Turner has been known to criticize his billionaire colleagues, especially the infamous Bill Gates, for not making the best use of their wealth. In 1997, he challenged Gates and others to match what he was doing: "I'm putting every rich person in the world on notice" (Turner, as cited in Brands, 1999, p. 291). He claimed that generosity wasn't something that had to hurt. His own net worth had grown from $2.2 billion to $3.2 billion in less than nine months, largely due to the increase in the value of his Time Warner stock. It comes easy, and it goes easy. "I'm not poorer than I was nine months ago, and the world is a lot better off" (Turner, as cited Brands, 1999, p. 291).

Critics of Turner cited this outlandish challenge as nothing more than a narcissistic outrage. They argued that it was just another eccentric episode from the antagonizing Turner. However, those who admired the billionaire felt that his generosity was such that Turner was actually accepting responsibility for the nation's welfare. They felt that he was not only sharing his fortune for the betterment of the entire nation, but that he was challenging other wealthy Americans to do the same.

"I've still got two billion left. Maybe I can make some more and give some more away later." —Ted Turner

During the 1990s, the usually volatile Turner appeared to be a much calmer and much more sedate individual. Apparently, this was due to psychological counseling as well as the prescription drug lithium (Hamilton, 1999).

A Risky Endeavor: TBS & Time Warner Merge

In 1996, Turner made one of his riskiest moves ever. He agreed to the merger of TBS and Time Warner. Gerald Levin, who was Time Warner's Chairman and Chief Executive, maintained his position. Turner, who had been at the helm of his company for more than two decades, surprisingly agreed to be second in command. He humorously noted, "I am married to Jane Fonda, so I know what it's like to be number two" (as cited in Current Biography Yearbook, 1998, p. 577).

When a reporter mentioned some past disagreements between TBS and Time Warner, Turner responded, "Now I'm Ted Time Warner. Hey, let's get the cash flow up, the stock price up, and live happily every after" (as cited in Brands, 1999, p. 289).

After the terms of the merger were hashed out, Turner's stock in TBS was transferred into stock of the new Time Warner. He instantly became the largest shareholder in the corporation, owning more than 11 percent of Time Warner. In Turner's new capacity, he was responsible for overseeing Time Warner's cable networks division. This was composed of Turner Broadcasting System's assets as well as HBO, Cinemax, and Time Warner's interest in cable channels Comedy Central and Court TV.

At the time of the merger, Ted was a self-proclaimed billionaire. But with every major merger comes personality clashes...and this merger was no different. Ted Turner kept quiet for a while, but it wasn't too long before the *Wall Street Journal* noted the following:

> A lot of people expected Mr. Turner would ride off into the sunset after he sold his Turner Broadcasting System Inc. to Time Warner. Instead, he is off on a wild ride through the world's biggest media empire, crashing into top executives' personal fiefdoms, abruptly canceling deals, asking impertinent questions about lavish expenses, and generally giving Time Warner a one-man dose of culture shock. (as cited in Brands, 1999, p. 289)

It was obvious that Turner had no intention of being a silent partner. In fact, he desperately wanted an active role within the organization. Turner had goals for the company; his primary reasons for agreeing to the merger with Time Warner included the following:

• To create the largest media conglomerate in the world.

• To gain access to Time Warner's library of films and cartoons. He knew that this important addition would significantly increase his own cable channels' range of programming.

- To gain easier access to limited cable channel space.

- To develop new programs in creative ways by combining the resources of the two companies. In 1996, for example, CNN/SI, a 24-hour news and sports network, was launched. (Current Biography Yearbook, 1998)

"My Greatest Regret"

Ted Turner suffered his greatest professional blow when CEO Gerald Levin announced the merger of Time Warner and AOL. Turner vehemently and, not surprisingly, outwardly expressed his opposition to the merger. His steadfast fight to prevent the merger was to no avail, however; the merger with AOL was finalized and announced on January 10, 2000.

Wall Street welcomed the announcement of the merger, and AOL Time Warner stock soared in price. Mr. Turner's fortune also soared since he was such a large shareholder in Time Warner. By the end of the day, his shares were worth $9 billion…$2.5 billion more than they were just one day prior to the merger.

This had no visible effect on Turner, however. He became furious when he was told that AOL Time Warner had written him out of its organizational operational flow chart. Levin and others believed that Mr. Turner would not be willing to make the necessary changes to meet the company's aggressive growth goals and strategic vision, and subsequently eliminated him from the corporate command of authority (Rutenberg & Stanley, 2001).

Never known for his verbal restraint, Turner lashed out at Levin to his fellow board members. To make his point more clearly heard by industry colleagues, Turner continued his criticism of Levin at a cable executive conference in November 2000. During this meeting, Turner told the audience that his biggest regret was selling his broadcasting empire to Time Warner in 1996 instead of buying the media giant (Rutenberg & Stanley, 2001).

"I could have fired Gerry Levin before he fired me." —Ted Turner

Apparently, Mr. Levin had enough of professional life and announced his upcoming resignation. After hearing this news, Turner responded with a sense of vindication. Some analysts have expressed a belief that it was Turner's criticism that ultimately convinced Mr. Levin to leave. Others, however, believe Turner had nothing to do with Levin's departure. One thing is for sure…Ted Turner was both bitter and depressed when he was pushed aside as a result of the AOL Time Warner merger. It was obvious that he felt personally betrayed by Mr. Levin.

Richard D. Parsons was elevated to the position of CEO of the merged companies. Initially there was widespread speculation that Turner would leave the new company after such a bitter ending to concentrate on his philanthropic foundation. One of Mr. Parson's first priorities as CEO, however, was to ask Ted Turner to continue on as Vice Chairman of the organization. This was a big gamble on Mr. Parson's part…given Turner's history of being notoriously outspoken and eccentric.

> Ted is my man. I love Ted. He knows more, particularly about the television space, which is at least a good third of this company. Ted and I have always had a wonderful relationship, and I am going to be reaching out to him, too. (Parsons, as cited in Mermigas, 2001)

Fay Vincent, an AOL Timer Warner director, former baseball commissioner, and friend of former Time Warner CEO Gerald Levin noted the following:

> Ted is a complicated guy, but he is part genius. Ted doesn't mean the harm he causes; he just cannot shut up. If he stays with us, one would hope he could be relatively loyal and not say anything he pleases. (Rutenberg & Stanley, 2001)

After much deliberation, Turner finally agreed to Parson's request and released a statement indicating his employment acceptance. "I'm very pleased to extend my contract as Vice Chairman of AOL Time Warner and I'm enthusiastic about working with Dick Parsons and the rest of the management team." (as cited in "AOL's Turner," 2001, p. B5)

A Subdued Ted Turner

Although a billionaire, Ted Turner has suffered several major setbacks in life. After the AOL Time Warner merger in 2001, he was denied control of the company that he had founded over 20 years earlier. To add injury to insult, his marriage to Jane Fonda ended. Even worse, his two-year-old granddaughter died suddenly of a rare hereditary disease.

Turner's business relationship with top brass at Time Warner, which bought Turner Broadcasting System in 1996, was damaged considerably after his role was severely limited when AOL and Time Warner merged.

As a result of that merger, Turner was stripped of his responsibilities for cable networks, and many members of his hand-picked management team were replaced.

Still owning 3.8% of all AOL Time Warner stock, he is a major shareholder. Down, but certainly not out, Turner recently told CNN executives, "Let's not forget we made a lot of money. Hundreds of millions of dollars. That's about all I have left is money, but if you're going to be left with something, that's better than a sharp stick in the eye" (Schwed, 2002).

The TBS, Inc. Timeline

Ted Turner's life, both personally and professionally, has been anything but routine. He has conquered some of life's greatest challenges, yet has also been dealt some very devastating blows. Below is a timeline of events, highlighting Turner's most significant accomplishments (Turner Broadcasting System, 2001b):

January 1, 1970: Atlanta independent UHF channel 17 (WJRJ) is purchased by Turner Communications Group and renamed WTCG.

January 3, 1976: Major League Baseball's Atlanta Braves purchased.

December 17, 1976: WTCG is beamed via satellite to cable homes nationwide, becoming cable's first Super station.

January 28, 1977: Turner Broadcasting System, Inc. purchases the National Basketball Association Atlanta Hawks.

August 21, 1979: Turner Communications Corporation changes its name to Turner Broadcasting System, Inc., and WTCG is renamed WTBS.

June 1, 1980: CNN, the world's first 24-hour, all-news network, premiers at 6 p.m. with 1.7 million subscribers.

January 1, 1982: Headline News premiers as CNN2 in more than 800,000 cable homes providing complete, updated newscasts every half-hour.

April 1983: Turner Learning is formed to develop, market and distribute Turner Broadcasting System programming to the nation's schools.

March 1984: CNN wins its first Peabody Award for Excellence in Programming.

July 5-20, 1986: Inaugural Goodwill games take place in Moscow.

October 3, 1988: Turner Network Television (TNT) debuts in 17 million cable homes—by far the largest network launch to date in cable history.

April 26, 1989: Turner Broadcasting System, Inc. announces plans for CNN Newsroom, a commercial-free program for use in the nations' junior and senior high schools.

April 3, 1990: CNN wins Peabody Award for its coverage of the Tienemen Square uprising in China.

July 20-August 5, 1990: Goodwill Games take place in Seattle.

January 16, 1991: Air assault of Operation Desert Storm begins. Worldwide audience of 1 billion people, largest in TV history for a non-sporting event, watches CNN's coverage.

January 28, 1991: Turner Broadcasting System, Inc. launches TNT Latin America.

October 17, 1991: Braves win the National League Pennant, and play in the first World Series since the club moved to Atlanta in 1966.

December 28, 1991: Time Magazine names Ted Turner 1991 Man of the Year.

October 1, 1992: Turner Broadcasting System, Inc. launches the Cartoon Network—the world's first 24-hour, all animation television service.

April 30, 1993: Turner Broadcasting System, Inc. launches the Cartoon Network in Latin America.

September 17, 1993: TNT and Cartoon Network launch in Europe.

January 28, 1994: Turner Broadcasting System, Inc. completes its acquisition of New Line Cinema, the leading independent producer and distributor of motion pictures.

July 23-August 7, 1994: More than 2000 of the world's finest athletes from 50 countries take part in the Goodwill Games in St. Petersburg, Russia.

October 6, 1994: Turner Broadcasting System, Inc. launches the first 24-hour cartoon and movie channel in the Asia Pacific region, Cartoon Network and TNT.

August 30, 1995: CNN launches an innovative, multimedia news service on the Internet becoming the only site with a full-time staff reporting news updated 24 hours a day.

September 22, 1995: Turner Broadcasting System, Inc. announces plans to merge with Time Warner Inc.

October 28, 1995: The Atlanta Braves win baseball's World Championship by defeating the Cleveland Indians 1-0 in game six of the World Series.

December 29, 1995: Turner Broadcasting System, Inc. launches CNNfn— The Financial Network.

October 10, 1996: Time Warner closes merger with Turner Broadcasting System, Inc. and names Ted Turner Vice Chairman, head of Time Warner's cable networks division.

December 10, 1996: CNN/Sports Illustrated, the 24-hour sports news network, is launched with 4.5 million subscribers.

March 17, 1997: CNN en Espanol, the 24-hour Spanish-language news network, is launched with 3.5 million viewers throughout Latin America.

June 25, 1997: The National Hockey League awards the city of Atlanta an expansion franchise; Turner Broadcasting forms the Atlanta Thrashers.

December 9, 1997: CNN Interactive launches CNNenEspanol.com, the first Spanish-language Website featuring breaking news.

July 19, 1998: More than 1300 athletes from over 70 countries compete in the 1998 Goodwill games in New York City.

October 1, 1999: Turner South, TBS, Inc.'s first regional entertainment network launches.

January 10, 2000: Time Warner announces merger with AOL.

April 1, 2000: Boomerang, Cartoon Network's classic cartoon channel, launches.

September 11, 2000: CNN Interactive launches CNNfyi.com for young people and educators.

September 21, 2000: CNN Interactive launches European-focused website.

December 2000: TBS Super station surpasses 80 million subscriber totals.

January 11, 2001: America Online and Time Warner Inc. complete merger to create AOL Time Warner.

January 2001: Turner Network Television surpasses 80 million subscriber totals.

February 2001: Cartoon Network surpasses 70 million subscriber totals.

April 2001: TCM reaches 50 million subscribers.

May 23, 2001: Gerald Levin resigns as CEO of AOL Time Warner; Richard Parsons becomes the new CEO.

June 29, 2001: Boomerang launches in Latin America.

August 6, 2001: CNN Headline News debuts new state-of-the-art studio.

Ted Turner as a Leader

Leadership is almost impossible to define because it changes so dramatically from situation to situation. A great wartime leader may not be a great leader in times of peace. Depending on circumstances, a monarch or dictator may be a great leader, or simply a despot who was born to a position of power.

Ted Turner is not a great leader because he is able to inspire others or because he is a peacemaker. On the contrary, he is a very bombastic, temperamental, and self-centered person. His leadership abilities consist of his extreme self-confidence, his willingness to take gambles, and his insistence on doing everything "his way." These characteristics may not make him a warm and loving person, but they have definitely helped him achieve dramatically positive financial results. Rightly or wrongly, positive financial results are one of the most common ways that leaders are measured and defined.

References

ABCNews.com (2001). *Reference.* New York: Author, Retrieved on February 11, 2002, from the World Wide Web: http://abcnews.go.com/reference/bios/turner.html

AOL's Turner signs contract to remain in current position. (2001, December 24). *Wall Street Journal* [eastern edition], p. B5.

Brands, H.W. (1999). *Masters of enterprise.* New York: Free Press.

Current biography yearbook. (1998). New York: The H.W. Wilson Company.

Hamilton, N. A. (1999). *American business leaders: From colonial times to the present* (vol. 2). Santa Barbara, CA: ABC-CLIO.

Mermigas, D. (2001, December 10). Parsons wants Ted back. *Electronic Media,* 20 (1), 23. Retrieved February 11, 2002, from ProQuest Direct database on the World Wide Web: http://proquest.umi.com

Rutenberg, J., & Stanley, A. (2001, December 16). At 63, Ted Turner may yet roar again. *New York Times* [late edition], p. 3.1. Retrieved February 11, 2002, from ProQuest Direct database on the World Wide Web: http://proquest.umi.com

Schwed, P. (2002, January 1). 100 most influential Georgians: R.E. (Ted) Turner. *Georgia Trend,* 17, 55. Retrieved February 11, 2002, from ProQuest Direct database on the World Wide Web: http://proquest.umi.com

Turner Broadcasting System. (2001a). *About TBS, Inc.: Corporate history* Atlanta, GA: Author, Retrieved on February 11, 2002, from the World Wide Web: http://www.turner.com/about/history.html

Turner Broadcasting System. (2001b). *About TBS, Inc.: Timeline* Atlanta, GA: Author, Retrieved on February 11, 2002, from the World Wide Web: http://www.turner.com/about/timeline.html

G. Richard Wagoner, Jr.

Chief Executive Officer
General Motors Corporation

"I like to get in the game. I'm not the kind of guy who likes to sit on the sidelines and coach. I like to play." —Richard Wagoner

The "Wagoner" Ride to the Top

Rick Wagoner was born in Wilmington, Delaware, on February 9, 1953. He was raised in Richmond, Virginia, and attended college at Duke University. At 6'4", Wagoner was, and still is, an avid basketball fan. In fact, he played freshman basketball at Duke University. He later earned an MBA from Harvard University, graduating in 1977. He currently resides in Bloomfield Hills, Michigan, a suburb of Detroit, with his wife and three sons.

Wagoner has spent his entire career with General Motors, and the majority of his career in finance positions. After completing his advanced degree at Harvard, he was hired in at General Motor's Treasurer's Office. He held numerous positions in the Treasurer's Office, including Manager of Latin American Financing, Director of Canadian and Overseas Borrowing, and Director of Capital Analysis and Investment.

In 1981, Wagoner moved to become Treasurer of GM Brasil in Sao Paulo. In 1984, he was promoted to Executive Director of Finance for that unit. In 1987, he returned to North America as Vice President and Finance Manager of GM of Canada Ltd. In October 1988, he became Group Director of Strategic Business Planning for the former Chevrolet-Pontiac-GM of Canada Group (Wagoner, 2001b).

Wagoner then added to his international expertise by serving as Vice President in charge of Finance for General Motors Europe, based in Zurich, Switzerland, from June 1989 to July 1991. His last international assignment was President and Managing Director of GM Brasil. In this capacity, Wagoner was credited with revitalizing and modernizing the product offerings (Wagoner, 2001b).

In addition to his rigorous business schedule, Wagoner serves as chairman of the Board of Visitors for his Alma Mater, Duke University's Fuqua School of Business; chairman of the Society of Automotive Engineers Vision 2000 Executive Committee; and a member of the Board of Trustees for Detroit Country Day School (Wagoner, 2001b).

Despite facing many obstacles and problems during his tenure at GM, he maintains a positive outlook. His philosophy is not to look at things as problems, but rather to consider them "opportunities." In his own candid style, Mr. Wagoner once noted, "Everything's not perfect. I've learned here that it's never going to be. But I feel better than ever. We don't see anything that's not fixable" (as cited in Nathan, 2000).

The Transfer of Leadership

Mr. Wagoner has obviously "fixed" the right things throughout his career at GM. On June 1, 2000, Mr. G. Richard Wagoner assumed the position of CEO of General Motors. At age 47, he was the youngest chief executive of General Motors since Billy Durant, who was the founder of the company back in 1908. Wagoner's appointment did not come without tough competition, however. He was competing for the number one position with another internal candidate, Harry Pearce, Vice Chairman overseeing Hughes Electronics and other non-automotive GM subsidiaries, as well as several outside candidates. Some of the outside competitors included such well known names as J.T. Battenberg III, Delphi Automotive Systems Chairman, and Michael Armstrong, AT&T Chairman (Anonymous, 2000).

Wagoner's predecessor, Jack Smith, has been credited with saving GM from possible bankruptcy. He slashed costs and reorganized the management structure. Under his leadership, the company proved to be both solid and profitable. When Smith was asked about his successor, he noted, "We have the finest CEO in the industry right here. Game over" (as cited in Haglund, 2000).

When Wagoner took over at the helm, he inherited an organization that had seen a dramatic turnaround. However, the organization still faced many challenges in an intensely global automotive environment. His primary task was to have General Motors reach a new level...and, more importantly, maintain that level.

Mr. Wagoner is a definite people person. His motivation and his ability to lead his employees are apparent in the following statement:

> I work well with people. I'm intellectually curious. I pick up things pretty quickly, defer to the experts, but I have reasonably high expectations. I don't as a practice go around kicking people in the rear end, but people need to perform, and I'm certainly not above chiding people for better performance.
>
> I'm all in favor of going fast, but the objective isn't going fast. The objective is having great products in the marketplace, doing the best job you can on market share, on quality and financials. So you go as fast as you can to achieve these objectives. I think the most important thing is you've got to work well with people in jobs like this; you've got to be a good judge of talent. (Hakim, 2001)

At the start, Mr. Wagoner's responsibilities did not change markedly, as he was already running the global automotive operations...GM's largest business. He did inherit two additional direct reports...the company's Chief Financial Officer and the head of GM's Finance Unit. Wagoner's top priorities as CEO have been to:

- Make the internal mechanisms at GM work together as one company
- Reduce internal conflict by acting as one company
- Take advantage of the global economy
- Speed up company decision-making and product development
- Intensify the focus on existing products (Wagoner, 2001c).

Wagoner also continued to spearhead GM's leap into the Internet. At the start of 1999, he challenged his staff to develop an e-commerce plan within 90 days. The result was the consolidation of GM's Internet activities under e-GM, partnerships with several dot.com companies, and an initiative to move all purchasing online (Wagoner, 2001c).

Promoting Youth

Throughout his years at General Motors, Wagoner has surrounded himself with his peers. Due to those who have left the company through retirement or other reasons, several top-level positions have become available. It did not take Wagoner long to promote some of his entourage. Some of the individuals who were promoted to executive positions at General Motors include the following:

- Mark Hogan: President of eGM. Hogan graduated with Wagoner from Harvard University's MBA school in 1978.

- John Smith: Vice President and General Manager of GM Service Parts Operations. Smith graduated from Harvard's MBA school in 1977.

- Larry Burns: Vice President of Research, Development and Planning. Burns has reported directly to Wagoner since 1996, as director of North American Product Planning.

- Mike Burns: President of GM Europe. Just as Wagoner, Burns started his career in the GM Treasurer's Office in New York (Miller, 2000).

Apparently, industry analysts are in favor of the changes. "I would like to see fresh blood from outside GM in the senior executive ranks," said David Bradley, an auto analyst with J.P. Morgan Securities. No doubt, he was impressed with Wagoner's selection of people to top-level management positions. Another analyst with Wasserstein Perella Securities also considered the changes as positive, "The view is that there has been a team approach at GM. And the captain of the team is leading in the right direction" (as cited in Miller, 2000).

John Smith, who actually came to know Wagoner through pickup basketball games at Harvard, notes the following about the man at the top, "Rick approaches everything with an incredible amount of energy. He's results-oriented, without question." He drew an analogy to the basketball court when he stated, "He was competitive, but more importantly he was a team player" (as cited in Miller, 2000).

Rick "The Coach"

In a recent speech in Orlando, Florida, Mr. Wagoner commented on the leadership culture at General Motors. He attempted to draw a parallel between General Electric and General Motors. He noted that GE stock performance was exceptional due to revenue growth, margins, and return on investment. He proclaimed that these results were achieved due to the leadership of the organization. They stretched for incredible results, they strove to reach them with a sense of urgency, they maintained high expectations of their leaders, and they didn't accept excuses.

His intent was to provoke the audience…truly get them excited about General Motors. He wholeheartedly believes in General Motors, and expects those people associated with GM to have the same conviction. He is extremely confident with the leadership, the products, the assets, and the GM alliance partners (Wagoner, 2000).

He believes in "stretch goals" and encourages all GM employees to develop personal stretch objectives. He assures them that he, too, has his own personal stretch targets established. Additionally, he has organizational stretch objectives. One example of these objectives, which he considers vision objectives, is a five-percent increase in net income. He feels that the current rate of improving net income is much too slow. Is this goal possible to reach? According to Wagoner it is, and the key is to reduce costs by three percent before taxes. This would result in a two percent after tax savings. If GM accomplished this, the five-percent target would be achieved instantaneously.

Mr. Wagoner has also instituted "go fast" sessions throughout the organization. These are sessions in which employees meet to develop strategies to move General Motors more quickly. The intent is to consider every process in which GM is involved. The employees consider everything from deciding which cars and trucks to build, to how to schedule executive appointments. The individuals involved in these sessions credit Wagoner for cutting approval times for Internet ventures from months to weeks (White, 2000).

Mr. Wagoner's employees also endorse his approach. One of his top lieutenants supports this notion with the following statement:

> Rick's a very nice combination of hands-on, very smart, and yet stands back and lets people get on with their jobs. We all have egos, and I know Rick does, but he can push his ego off to the side, and that helps. (as cited in Hakim, 2002)

The Definition of "Great"

"When I meet my business school friend a few years from now, at our 30-year reunion, I want her to say to me, 'You're still working for GM? That's a great company.'" —Richard Wagoner

According to Wagoner, the definition of "great" is somewhat in the eye of the beholder, and is subject to change with the times. He has attempted to define greatness, however, with the following comments:

To me, General Motors will be great...

- when every employee in General Motors, everywhere in the world, is allowed—no, encouraged—to feel like he or she can contribute to the maximum of their capabilities.

- when we have taken full advantage of the opportunity that diversity offers us.

- when we work seamlessly with our partners for our mutual success.

- when we fulfill our potential in China and India, and other growing markets around the world.

- when we are on the leading edge of innovation—in cars and trucks, in new products, in services, in things that we can't even imagine.

- when we identify new business opportunities and go after them, fast.

- when we are respected by our suppliers, our dealers, our unions, and other institutions, as being demanding and tough, but fair—always fair.

- when we are recognized by our communities around the world as the automotive leader on environmental issues.

- when our sales and market share are climbing in every market around the world.

- when we lead in quality.

- when our customers say, "GM—that's a company I trust; that's a company I want to do business with."

- when acting as one company, stretch, sense of urgency, product and customer focus are ingrained in our every thought and action. (Wagoner, 2000)

Rick Wagoner would probably be the first to admit that the above descriptions of greatness are idealistic and almost impossible to attain in every aspect. But when you believe in stretch goals...when you believe that people can and do respond to challenges...then your job as a leader is to set the goals high and expect the best efforts of your people.

September 11, 2001...When the World Changed

September 11, 2001 was the opening day of the Frankfurt Motor Show in Germany. Rick Wagoner was in attendance at the show and was conducting media interviews following a press conference in which General Motors unveiled new vehicles. It was a festive day filled with joy and excitement...until word got out as to what had transpired in New York, Washington, and Pennsylvania. Immediately, the atmosphere changed, and the mood of the show suddenly turned somber. Attendees scrambled to nearby television sets to listen in on the latest news briefs.

It was several days before Wagoner made it back to the United States; and shortly after his return, he was scheduled to give a talk to The Executives' Club of Chicago. He used that speech to talk about his personal reactions to the events of September 11, and made the following comments:

> One of the things that really struck me while we worked and waited in Europe for our chance to return to the States was how swiftly and how intently the world reached out to us, as Americans. The outpouring of support from our colleagues in Germany, and throughout Europe, was simply incredible.

> Then, after arriving home, I was again moved by the many personal messages of sympathy, support, and solidarity I had received from our GM business partners—dealers, suppliers, joint-venture partners, and even competitors—from around the globe.

> It was extraordinary for me to realize that an act of terrorism that was so purposely aimed at breaking our spirit apart, had actually served to draw us closer together—and I'm not just talking about America. I mean virtually the whole world. (Wagoner, 2001a)

Wagoner further noted that times of crisis require strong leadership. He said that local communities and the country as a whole needed leadership. President Bush was doing his part, and it was time for General Motors and its employees to step up to the plate. He already had his team working on ideas about how General Motors could help...but he wasn't ready to unveil those ideas just yet.

The General Motors' Plan

Immediately after the attack, General Motors hosted a meeting with a group of business, labor, and government leaders to discuss what collectively could be done in wake of the September 11 tragedy. The general consensus was that it was important to strive to keep the American economy as strong as ever. It was critical to keep workers employed, keep factories functioning, keep the economy growing, and ultimately keep our nation thriving.

In the American spirit, General Motors introduced the "Keep America Rolling" campaign. It was a bold move on the part of the largest United States automaker...but it worked. It helped stimulate the economy by making it easier and more affordable for Americans to purchase vehicles. The company introduced 0% financing on every single GM car and truck...for a minimum of 36 months and, in some instances, for as long as 60 months. This was an unprecedented move by General Motors...one that was later copied by rival competitors DaimlerChrysler and Ford Motor Company. The primary goal of this particular campaign was to help rebuild consumer confidence...which it succeeded in doing...but it was also a master marketing stroke for General Motors. With this program, GM not only helped America, it helped itself by regaining some of the market share that it has lost in previous years.

Three Critical Aspects of Leadership at General Motors

Mr. Wagoner believes that business executives...from all areas of business...have the responsibility to answer the call for leadership during times of crisis. In an attempt to assist in the revitalization of the economy, Wagoner and his staff have focused in on three specific areas of leadership...engaging, prioritizing, and commitment to innovation (Wagoner, 2001a).

Engaging

At GM, I've been telling our executives that we need to lead in two ways right now—we need to engage our employees by helping them regain their balance and, following that, we need to engage our company in the economic turnaround of the U.S.

With regard to our employees, we know they're back at work, determined to do their part, to make sacrifices—but like all Americans, they're grieving, they're angry, they're nervous, and they're distracted. And they're looking for leadership more than ever. That's why we're working overtime to reassure them that our facilities are secure, that our foremost priority is their safety, and that we understand that everyone is dealing with this tragedy, both at home and at work.

Prioritizing

Our first priority is a commitment to our people. Part of that commitment is a promise to keep our company healthy and strong. And that leads us to ask some tough questions—to re-evaluate virtually everything we do. Is it important? Is it critical? Can we do it better? Can we do without it?

We need to re-evaluate our priorities throughout the company, and shelve—temporarily or permanently—the projects and initiatives that are not essential to the success of the business. Not only does this cause us to focus on what is most important to the success of our company, it also helps our employees streamline their jobs at a time when many of them continue to struggle with the emotional effects of the crisis.

In short, we're stepping back from business as usual, prioritizing our needs, and working to make sure we take care of the big issues first—because those are the issues critical to the success of our business, and our nation's economy.

Commitment to Innovation

One of the qualities that has made America the most productive nation on earth is our ability to innovate—to take risks. Our inclination in uncertain times is often to hunker down and avoid risk—but we need to resist that urge, and do what we do best: innovate and improve.

At GM, for example, we've built our reputation—and our continuing 70-year run atop the global auto industry—first and foremost, because of our commitment to innovation. We're proud of that history—but, of course, we can't operate in the past. As Thomas Jefferson put it, "The past is a good place to visit, but you wouldn't want to live there."

My point is simply this: just as innovation got GM to the number one position in the global auto business—innovation has propelled the U.S. to be the most productive nation on earth. And it's innovation that will enable us to maintain that position in the years to come.

Obstacles That Still have to be Overcome

Rick Wagoner has made great strides in turning General Motors into the type of company that he wants it to be...the type of company that he believes it can be. But his work is far from complete, and there are several challenges that still remain. Mr. Wagoner is acutely aware of these obstacles, and he has been steadily working to overcome them. Listed below are some of the major challenges that GM faces as well as the steps which Wagoner has taken to resolve the issues:

Challenge: Very few GM products appeal to people under age sixty.

Solution: Hire Bob Lutz, the dynamic ex-Chrysler leader who spearheaded some of Chrysler's most successful new products. Lutz is in a position of power where his ideas will be executed and his management style will be practiced.

Challenge: Union/Management relationship is less than desirable.

Solution: Realize that this problem was years in the making and can't be solved overnight. Appoint people who know how to deal with unions and have them work on long-term relationships. Resolve to treat union employees with respect, but also resolve not to "give away the store" in negotiations.

Challenge: Competition...both domestic and foreign...has been a continual struggle.

Solution: Two-fold. Increase emphasis on product quality throughout the organization and emphasize new and exciting designs that will make people want to buy the products.

Challenge: General Motors has a reputation for being extremely complex, highly bureaucratic and extremely political.

Solution: Acknowledge the truth of this reputation and start changing the organization from the top down. Lead by example, and keep meeting and decision chains short. Hire knowledgeable outsiders to shake up the ingrown bureaucracy.

Ongoing Challenges

Although Mr. Wagoner has been quite successful with his Internet ventures, not all have gone off without a hitch. Some insiders express concern that the company's bureaucracy is not comfortable working on Internet time…as opposed to annual budgets and quarterly sales forecasts. Wagoner, himself, concedes that too much focus on new technology could distract GM from its core business: making cars. According to Wagoner, "The challenge is how do you cheerlead for the new stuff and not imply that you're leaving the auto stuff behind" (White, 2000).

Another area of concern for the number one automobile manufacturer is that of market share. Despite record profits, GM's market share had been slipping consistently…right up until the "Keep America Rolling" campaign that broke after the terrorist attacks. This promotion gave GM a small surge in market share…but Wagoner still faced criticism. His critics said that GM was simply "buying" market share, and some even suggested that the highly successful campaign was somewhat "tacky," since it came about as a result of a national disaster. Wagoner and his fellow GM executives dismiss this as "sour grapes," but the fact remains that GM's slight increase in U.S. market share came at great cost. GM's future success will depend on maintaining and increasing U.S. market share by less expensive means. Additionally, they will have to fight for market share in Europe because GM's European operations, plagued in the past few years by quality problems and intense competition, have lost ground as well.

Another disappointment for Mr. Wagoner has been the Saturn L-Series. It was intended to be the vehicle that would help turn things around in the United States. Mr. Wagoner felt that the vehicle could capitalize on

GM's ability to marshal global resources (the L-Series is based on an Opel chassis) and develop a well-known brand, in this case Saturn, into a low-cost line of reliable compact cars popular for its no-haggle pricing policy.

However, GM's efforts to execute this strategy ran into trouble early on. In development, the car sparked feuding among engineers who had never worked together before. Senior executives would routinely intervene to settle disputes. Even minor design features created friction. For example, German engineers were at odds with the American market's desire for a cup holder large enough to accommodate Big Gulp drinks that have become increasingly popular in the American market (White, 2000).

There were more significant issues at hand as well. Saturn considers safety one of the core values of its brand. Consequently, its executives were confident that the vehicle would receive top safety ratings across the board on government crash tests. Unfortunately, it received only one top rating out of four (White, 2000).

When production finally began, culture clashes continued. U.S. engineers discovered that their German counterparts had slightly different specifications for many of the variables that make it possible for a car's parts to work together. Plastic parts in the interior did not fit, nor did the body panels coming from Saturn's flagship plant in Tennessee (White, 2000).

The actual launch of the vehicle was obviously very difficult. The L-Series' slow start-up resulted in dealers not having sufficient vehicles to sell. By the time the plant reached full production, it was months behind schedule. To make matters worse, sales had declined sharply. Subsequently, Saturn was forced to cut production and announce layoffs for the first time.

GM's top brass assures analysts and shareholders that they know how to avoid these major pitfalls in the future. But knowing what to do, and being able to do it, are two separate issues. Rick Wagoner knows that the problems encountered in the Saturn launch may be indicative of future problems that GM will have to solve if it is to become a true "world" company.

The Road to Success for General Motors

"We want to challenge the conventional wisdom of GM."
—Richard Wagoner

General Motors' executives...led by Rick Wagoner...are attempting to promote a business model that is new, exciting and fast-moving...ready to take on the new economy. To prove they are making progress in achieving this model, Wagoner now proudly proclaims:

- There are chief information officers in all business units.

- Since 1996, GM has hired more than 200 e-business experts with a turnover of only 2 or 3 percent.

- Since 1997, GM has hired more than 300 top managers from outside the company.

- GM has 10 families of gasoline engines plus five families of diesels and 80 percent of GM's engines will be all new or significantly upgraded by 2003.

- Global alliances give the GM network 24 percent of global sales, including 30 percent in Latin America, 18 percent in Asia-Pacific, 20 percent in Europe and 30 percent in North America.

GM Targets Defined by Mr. Wagoner

In keeping with his theory of setting stretch objectives, Mr. Wagoner has set out the following ambitious objectives for General Motors:

- Raise global market share, including sales of affiliates, to 28 percent from current 24 percent.

- Average 15 percent return on net assets.

- Average 5 percent return on sales.

- Make 50 percent of new products create new niches or segments.

- Achieve 18-month or less vehicle-development time, from verified data release to start of production.

- By 2004, average close to zero lost days of production per changeover.

- Reduce inventory in pipeline, from factory to dealer lots, by 50 percent.

In a recent presentation, Mr. Wagoner summed up the future of General Motors by making the following remarks (Wagoner, 2001c):

In general I think it's fair to say we compete in a world marked by competitive markets, excess capacity, and a growing number of strong, global competitors. The price pressure it tough...and it's only going to grow more intense. In this situation, how can we distinguish ourselves in the eyes of our customers? I believe there's one clear way...innovation. Without it, no company lasts for long. And that's exactly why I've put "innovative products and services" at the top of my list of business priorities for General Motors.

References

Anonymous. (2000, March 18). Face value: GM's motor man. *The Economist*, 354 (8162), 69. Retrieved January 16, 2002, from ProQuest Direct database on the World Wide Web: http:// proquest.umi.com

Haglund, R. (2000, February 3). Wagoner promises to make the GM nimbler. *The Grand Rapids Press*, p. B5. Retrieved January 16, 2002, from ProQuest Direct database on the World Wide Web: http:// proquest.umi.com

Hakim, D. (2001, November 25). 'Type B' chief guides GM on a course to revival. *The New York Times*, p. 3.1. Retrieved January 28, 2002, from ProQuest Direct database on the World Wide Web:http:// proquest.umi.com

Lapham, E. (2000, July 3). Wagoner definitely in charge at GM. *Automotive News*, 14. Retrieved January 28, 2002, from ProQuest Direct database on the World Wide Web: http://proquest.umi.com

Miller, J. (2000, June 5). Wagoner: We must move at Internet speed. *Automotive News*, 8. Retrieved January 28, 2002, from ProQuest Direct database on the World Wide Web: http://proquest.umi.com

Nathan, S. (2000, February 3). Upbeat Wagoner known as team player. *USA Today*, 03B. Retrieved January 16, 2002, from ProQuest Direct database on the World Wide Web: http://proquest.umi.com

Wagoner, G. R. Jr. (2000, September 19). Speech given at the General Motors Global Leadership Conference, Orlando, FL. Retrieved on January 27, 2002, from General Motors' Intranet.

Wagoner, G. R. Jr. (2001a, September 27). Keep America rolling. Speech given at The Executives' Club of Chicago, Chicago, IL. Retrieved on January 27, 2002, from General Motors' Intranet.

Wagoner, G. R. Jr. (2001b, June 5). Speech given at the Ninety-third Annual Meeting of Stockholders at Hotel duPont, Wilmington, DE. Retrieved on January 27, 2002, from General Motors' Intranet.

Wagoner, G. R. Jr. (2001c, April 28). Speech given to the GM Supplier of the Year Awards, Washington, D.C. Retrieved on January 27, 2002, from General Motors' Intranet.

White, G. (2000, July 11). Core issues: As GM courts the Net, struggling Saturn line exposes rusty spots...global campaign to develop a mid size series yielded infighting and dull design...new stuff vs. 'auto stuff.' *The Wall Street Journal*, A.1. Retrieved January 28, 2002, from ProQuest Direct database on the World Wide Web: http:// proquest.umi.com

Jack Welch
Former Chairman and CEO
General Electric Company

"Good business leaders create a vision, articulate the vision, passionately own the vision, and relentlessly drive it to completion." —Jack Welch

Jack Welch has been described as one of, if not the best, corporate leaders of the 20th century. He has been called the CEO's CEO and the gold standard by which all CEOs are to be measured. During the 20 years that he was CEO, General Electric experienced unprecedented growth and a phenomenal return on investment for its shareholders. Thanks to Jack Welch, GE is widely regarded as one of the best-managed and profitable corporations in the world. Jack Welch holds the unique distinction of having created more shareholder value than such corporate leaders as: Gates, Eisner, Buffett, Walton, or Grove (Byrne, 1998).

The Early Years

John (Jack) Francis Welch, Jr. was born in 1935 in Salem, Massachusetts. He grew up in a working class family. While in high school, he was the captain of the hockey team (Murray, 2001). After high school, he went to the University of Massachusetts where he received a B.S. degree in chemical engineering in 1957. He then went on to continue his education at the University of Illinois. There, he received a M.S. 1958 and a Ph.D. in 1960. Both of the graduate degrees were in chemical engineering. That same year, he joined General Electric. GE would be his only place of employment for the next 41 years. In just twelve years, he became a Vice President. Five years later, in 1979, he became the Vice-Chair. Then, in 1981, he became the eighth Chairman and CEO of GE. He replaced Reginald Jones. He was the youngest person to have held the CEO position and he also held this position for the longest time, 20 years. He retired in September 2001 (Executive Bios).

Corporate Leadership

> *"You can't grow long-term, if you can't eat short-term.*
> *Anybody can manage short. Anybody can manage long.*
> *Balancing those two things is what management is."*
> —Jack Welch

During his tenure, Welch would turn GE into a very different company from the one he inherited. While GE's area of expertise had always been manufacturing, Welch would move GE into some very new territory: entertainment and finance. In 1986, GE acquired RCA, which included the NBC television network. He changed GE from being an old-style manufacturer into a very diversified international conglomerate. This transformation took place as a result of 993 separate acquisitions valued at over $130 billion and the selling of 408 GE businesses valued at $10.6 billion (Murray, 2001). Under Welch's leadership, GE would become the most valuable and profitable company in the world.

What is truly amazing about Welch's tenure is the incredible and consistent performance of GE. Since 1981, there were twenty consecutive years of dividend increases and a 25 percent increase in the value of the GE stock each and every year that Welch was the CEO. The cumulative increase, including dividends, during Welch's tenure was a phenomenal 5,096 percent. In Welch's first year, GE was the seventh-largest company in the country with a market capitalization of $13 billion. In 1987, GE became the first corporation to be valued at more than $200 billion. In 1991, GE surpassed IBM as the nation's most valued corporation. By July 1998, its shares had risen in value another $100 billion to $300 billion. When he retired in 2001, GE was the number one company in America with a market capitalization at about $400 billion (Murray, 2001).

Not surprisingly, Welch was handsomely rewarded for his corporate leadership. In 1999, Welch was paid $13.3 million, with $3.3 million of that in salary and $10 million as a bonus (Jack Welch Earns). In his last full year as the GE CEO he received a compensation package totaling $120 million (Murray, 2001).

Management Style

Jack Welch's accomplishments were especially remarkable when you consider how diverse the GE empire was in terms of the number of employees, the varied products and services and the multi-national locations. GE has $304 billion in assets, $89.3 billion in sales, and 276,000 employees in more than 100 countries (Byrne, 1998). Jack Welch's ability to successfully run GE for twenty years can be traced to four areas:

* Lead By Example

* Run It Like a Small Business

* Have a Clear Vision

* Develop Your Management Team

Lead by Example

From his earliest days at GE, Jack Welch thoroughly immersed himself in the work. He learned the job inside out. "An admitted workaholic who loved putting in days of 12 hours or more and in dragging home binders of stuff to read at night, he demanded the same commitment from others" (Murray, 2001). Throughout his tenure as CEO, he was known for his attention to details.

He was a very assertive hands-on leader who brought both charisma and enthusiasm to the CEO job. This style was a marked contrast to the stodgy Reginald Jones, the previous CEO. Welch's high-powered approach had the effect of bringing out the best in his employees. He was a no-nonsense boss who expected the same in return.

"When Welch speaks, he tells it to you straight." (Lowe, 1998)

"He is rarely indecisive. Welch will say yes. Welch will say no. But he never says maybe." (Byrne, 1998)

To keep his managers on their toes, Welch would frequently make unscheduled visits to GE plants for a "friendly" visit.

Run It Like a Small Business

"The best big companies try to think like small ones."

Welch's approach to managing the GE conglomerate was to run it like a small company. Small companies are able to respond to market changes rapidly with little bureaucratic interference. Welch envisioned GE with a small-company management philosophy but with big-company resources. Welch openly hated bureaucracy. During his entire tenure as CEO, he would be fighting against big-company bureaucracy.

"Keep it simple; face reality; embrace change; fight bureaucracy."

Welch was largely successful in his war on bureaucracy. Compared to other large companies, GE was able to move more rapidly into new products and industries.

Welch felt that one way to achieve an entrepreneurial atmosphere was by making the operational climate informal. In fact, everyone called the GE CEO "Jack." Welch felt that informality would facilitate the operation by speeding up communication up and down as well as across the GE chain of command (Byrne, 1998).

Have A Clear Vision

Shortly after Welch became the new CEO, he made his vision very clear:

"GE should be No. 1 or No. 2 in all businesses or get out of them."

This was obviously very controversial, but there is no denying that this vision was clearly understood by all. Those divisions that were marginal relative to the market would be either shut down or sold. This certainly got the attention of the managers.

Welch understood that in an organization as large as GE, the message needs to be relatively simple and it needs to be reinforced regularly and at all levels.

Develop Your Management Team

Welch was not able to manage GE by himself. He had an outstanding cadre of first-rate executives throughout the organization. He set in place a structure that would continually develop his management team. The formula for successful executive development was a combination of training, evaluating and rewarding. One of the reasons GE was so successful during Welch's reign was that the company had a first rate management team. One of Welch's priorities was to develop world class executive managers.

Jack Welch saw the training of the future leaders of the company as one of his most important roles as CEO. He devoted a large part of his time to executive training. There were two major training programs in which Welch played an active role. The first was the senior executive training session for GE's top 500 executives. This took place in Boca Raton, Florida each January. The other training session was for the up-and-coming junior executives. This was held each month in Croton-on-the-Hudson, New York. It was quite an honor to be picked for this program. This training program was valuable because it served as a vehicle to transfer "best practices" among GE's very diverse businesses (Byrne, 1998). Welch's favorite part of this training session was to field questions from the floor.

Evaluating

Although only 20 people directly reported to Welch, he closely monitored the performance of the top 600 GE managers. Welch encouraged very candid evaluations of his people.

...The greatest cruelty to employees is to lie in your performance appraisals...

...I call that "false kindness." In our company we let every employee know where they rank against each other. Letting them know late in life that they are no good is the ultimate management cruelty. (Savvy Advice, 1999)

To Welch, all employees fit into one of four categories.

Jack Welch's People Matrix

Competent and Buy In *Keep These*	Competent but Don't Buy In *Problem Creators! Nurture or Get Rid of*
Incompetent but Buy In *Train These*	Incompetent but Don't Buy In *Get Rid of These*

The best employees are those that are both competent and they buy into the company's goals and its culture. To Welch:

> *"Employees must share your basic values. They must buy into what you stand for. You can't keep people who don't, because one person who doesn't buy in can cause chaos."*

To Welch, the employees that present the greatest challenge are those in quadrant two.

> *"You must get them to buy in or get rid of them, no matter how good they are, because you can't have people who are not committed to what you stand for."*

Rewarding

While Welch always had very ambitious performance goals, he believed that those who deliver should be handsomely rewarded. While there may be an overall target salary increase of four percent, the top performing employees could have base salaries rise by as much as 25 percent in a year. Cash bonuses could increase by as "much as 150% in a year, to between 20% and 70% of base pay. Stock options, once reserved for the most senior officers at GE, have been broadly expanded under Welch. Now, some 27,000 employees get them, nearly a third of GE's professional employees" (Byrne, 1998).

Neutron Jack

Shortly after Jack Welch took over as the CEO, he went about "restructuring" the company to make it more competitive. Welch set out to eliminate unnecessary layers of management and to close unprofitable sites. Many of the operations were moved to overseas locations that had lower labor rates. Between 1981 and the mid-1990s, this downsizing process resulted in the elimination of more than 180,000 jobs, a quarter of GE's workforce. This was accomplished through a combination of layoffs and forced/early retirements (Murray, 2001). As a result, Welch was not an especially popular CEO with the unions and middle managers. Welch's slash-and-burn personnel policy earned him the nickname of "Neutron Jack." This may help to explain why, in 1984, *Fortune* magazine called Welch "the toughest boss in America."

"You have to destroy your own company to survive."

"Fix, close or sell."

Welch felt that these drastic actions were necessary if GE was going to remain profitable and competitive. While other large corporations had downsizings that were far more ruthless, Welch took a great deal of negative heat primarily because he was the first CEO to do what had to be done. Welch asserts that his proactive and aggressive actions were necessary and that they actually saved GE jobs in the long run. He contends that the layoffs would have been far more severe if he had waited.

"Change before you have to."

"What I did then compared to what's been done in the revolutions at IBM, GM, and other places was toy stuff."

Criticism

Many people (mostly non-CEOs) downplay Welch's success. "It is easy to be a CEO in boom times of the '90s." In other words: Welch was simply at the right place at the right time. However, Welch actually did much better than the market average. From 1995 to 2000, the value of GE shares rose by 331.69 percent. This compares to a 105.8 percent increase

for the Dow Jones Industrial Average, and a 121 percent increase for the
S&P 500 over the same period (GE names Immelt).

Although Welch outwardly professed to be concerned about both the
short and long-term performance, critics contend that performance in the
near term was all that really mattered to Neutron Jack. "No matter how
many records are broken in productivity or profits, it's always 'What have
you done for me lately?'" This pressure to perform created a climate that
some will say encouraged managers to cut corners. There were two major
scandals during Welch's tenure. The first had to do with defense contract-
ing and the other was the Kidder, Peabody & Co. bond-trading scheme of
the early 1990s (Byrne, 1998).

Up Close and Personal

Jack Welch remarried in 1989 to Jane Beasley. She was 36 and a lawyer by trade. Jack, at 53, was 17 years her senior. He met Jane six months
after he divorced his first wife of 28 years. Jack and his first wife had four
children.

As Welch was about to retire from GE in 2001, he was interviewed for
a *Harvard Business Review* article by Suzy Wetlaufer, the editor-in-chief.
Shortly thereafter, they became romantically involved. Welch at 66 was
still married to Jane, and Wetlaufer, at 42, was divorced. When the affair
was made public in March 2002, Jane Welch announced that she was
filing for divorce (Bandler, 2002). Since Jack and Jane had a very unusual
prenuptial agreement that expired after three years of marriage, Jack stands
to lose about $500 million in the divorce settlement (Jones, 2002).

The Welch Legacy

Although Jack Welch is now retired from GE, he plans to stay active
in the consulting business. He will advise active CEOs on how to be a
better corporate leader. He certainly has some very impressive creden-
tials for this job:

- "Manager of the Century"—*Fortune Magazine*

- "The gold standard against which other CEOs are measured"
  —*Business Week*

- "The most acclaimed CEO in the world"

- "One of the two greatest corporate leaders of the 20th century" (the other being Alfred Sloan of General Motors).

- "Bestselling Author"—his autobiography, *Jack, Straight From the Gut* was on the bestseller lists of the *New York Times*, Amazon.com, the *Wall Street Journal* and the Association of Independent Booksellers (Executive Bios).

Here is a sampling of some of the advice that he is likely to give to the CEOs:

"There are no bounds to human creativity."

"The idea flow from the human spirit is absolutely unlimited. All you have to do is tap into that well."

"I don't like to use the word efficiency. It's creativity. It's a belief that every person counts."

"If the customer isn't satisfied, if the stuff is getting stale, if the shelf isn't right, or if the offerings aren't right, it's the same thing."

"The people who get into trouble in our company are those who carry around the anchor of the past."

"Don't manage, lead."

"I never associate passion with the word manager, and I've never seen a leader without it."

"Face reality as it is, not as it was, or as you wish it to be."

"What counts is what you deliver."

"Be candid with everyone."

"If you don't have a competitive advantage, don't compete."

"Control your own destiny, or someone else will."

References

Bandler, J. (2002, April 25). Wetlaufer announces resignation from
  Harvard Business Review. The Wall Street Journal Online. Retrieved
  June 17, 2002, from wysiwyg://9/http://online.wsj.com/public/
  article_print/0,SB1019664323438237680,00.html

Byrne, J. (1998, June 8). How Jack Welch runs GE. *Business Week.*
  Retrieved July 20, 2002, from http://www.businessweek.com/1998/
  23/b3581001.htm

Executive Bios: Jack F. Welch Jr. (n.d.). Retrieved June 17, 2002, from
  http://www.ge.com/news/exec_office/printable/printable_welch2.html.

GE names Immelt to succeed Jack Welch. (2000, November 28).
  Rediff.com. Retrieved April 8, 2002, from http://www.rediff.com/
  money/2000/nov/28ge.htm

Jack Welch Earns $17m in salary, bonus. (2001, March 12).
  The Economic Times. Retrieved April 8, 2002, from http://
  www.economictimes.com/120301/12tech17.htm

Jack Welch's people matrix. (2000, October). Retrieved July 20, 2002,
  from http://www.bss-gn.com/nl/oct2000/art001.htm

Jones, D. (2002, March 12). Welch's wife seeks half of fortune in
  divorce. *USA Today*, B2.

Lowe, J. (1998). *Jack Welch speaks.* Retrieved July 20, 2002, from
  http://hallbiography.com/general/85.shtml

Murray, M. (2001, September 5). Why Jack Welch's brand of leadership
  matters. *The Wall Street Journal*, B10.

Savvy advice from Jack Welch. (1999, December 28). *Asia Pacific
  Management News.* Retrieved July 20, 2002, from
  www.apmforum.com/news/ap281299.htm

Welch, J. (2001). *Jack—Straight from the gut.* New York: Warner Books.

Oprah Winfrey
Chief Executive Officer
Harpo Entertainment Group

"I want people to have the grandest vision for their lives."
—Oprah Winfrey

Oprah...the Early Days

Oprah Gail Winfrey was born January 29, 1954. Her name was actually Orpah, a name that came from the Bible's book of Ruth. Although her birth certificate reads Orpah, most people did not know how to pronounce it. People generally reversed two of the letters, thus creating the name "Oprah" (Brands, 1999).

Oprah's biological mother, Vernita Lee, did not marry Oprah's father, Vernon Winfrey. In fact, it was Oprah's grandparents who raised Oprah. Her grandmother was actually known to Oprah as "Mommy."

Oprah's mother had multiple relationships throughout her lifetime. During some of these relationships, she would ask to have Oprah return to live with her. Although she preferred not to reside with her mother, Oprah was forced to acquiesce. Yet, each time, Oprah never stayed for a long period of time. During one of her extended stays with her mother, Oprah's life would be scarred forever. When her mother left for work, Oprah was often left with an older male cousin. She always felt very uncomfortable being in the young man's presence. It was during one of these days that her cousin would rape her. Oprah was told by the cousin never to say a word; if she were to say something, both of them would be in terrible trouble. Oprah agreed never to divulge anything. Unfortunately, this was not the only rape that would occur. Oprah was repeatedly raped in her own home by people who would visit her family. These terrible crimes resulted in Oprah possessing horribly low self-esteem...something that has had a deep effect on her to this day (Brands, 1999).

Throughout her troubled youth, Oprah would always have a refuge. She would turn to books as a safe haven. She was, and still is, an avid reader. Reading gave her hope and gave her the will to aspire to new goals. Oprah was exceptionally intelligent. Her strong intellect allowed her to skip both kindergarten and second grade. Oprah always praised her teachers for their guidance and support throughout her early years.

Although Oprah lived with a myriad of people throughout her lifetime, she credits her grandmother for making her the success that she is today. This is primarily because her grandmother acted as the dominant support figure during her youth. It was her grandmother, and later her father, who were the ones who expected the best out of her; they expected her to excel with everything she did. Time would prove this to be an expectation that was ultimately conquered.

Adolescent Problems

Oprah's academic success was not enough to prevent personal struggles. She was continually ridiculed for being an African American. In an effort to gain attention and affection, she became sexually active. This ultimately resulted in a teenage pregnancy; the baby was born prematurely and died shortly thereafter. Oprah would eventually end up moving back with her father and stepmother. These two individuals were strict and wanted desperately for Oprah to change her lifestyle. They expected Oprah to study endlessly and allowed her to watch television for only one hour a day...the local and national news (Raatma, 2001).

When Oprah started high school, integration was in its initial stages. It was then that Oprah experienced racism first hand. Instead of accepting racism, she attempted to change it. Her efforts were not in vain. With the help of teachers, family, and close friends, Oprah changed her life for the positive. During her senior year, Oprah was voted most popular student by her fellow classmates. She was clearly on her way to success.

Start to Fame

Oprah's celebrity status can be traced back to her high school days. She was offered a part-time position after school and on the weekends...reading the news on the radio. Her father worried that this would interfere with her studies; Oprah proved him wrong.

Oprah was invited to participate in a local beauty pageant. Her beauty along with her articulate speaking ability assisted in her winning several pageants. One such victory earned her a four-year scholarship to Tennessee State University.

During her sophomore year at college, she was encouraged to apply for a position at WTVF, a CBS television station in Nashville. When it came time to audition, her strategy was to imitate her idol, Barbara Walters. The technique was a success, and she was offered the job (Raatma, 2001).

While in her senior year in college, another position became available to Oprah. This job, as a reporter and co-anchor for the evening news, would require her to move to Baltimore, Maryland. She decided to take the venture. Her father was disappointed that she did not complete college, but she vowed that she would be back to finalize her studies.

She had mixed reviews in her new position. Some people felt that she was too emotional for the job. Her critics said that she would sometimes mispronounce words because she preferred to report impromptu as opposed to following a script. Since the station had signed a long-term contract with Oprah, they felt that they would find a new position for her. In 1977, a new station manager approached Oprah with yet another proposition. He decided to start a talk show titled *People are Talking*. This program would resemble the then most prominent television talk show available...Phil Donahue. The format of the program would allow members of the audience to participate in the show. It would be hosted by two individuals...a male and female (Brands, 1999).

People are Talking would eventually beat Donahue in the Baltimore television ratings. The show was soon picked up in other cities across the United States. Oprah was becoming a well-known television personality.

Problems Associated with Success

Oprah was becoming a true icon of success professionally; but her personal life suffered. She had serious problems with relationships that evolved throughout the years. Her self-esteem was exceptionally low. When she developed a seemingly strong relationship with a member of the opposite sex, she felt obsessed with being with the person at all times. Her insecurity and lack of self-confidence clearly was due to her childhood experiences. Gayle King, her best friend and now editor of *O, The Oprah Magazine*, was always by her side offering words of encouragement. To this day, they still remain the best of friends.

A.M. Chicago

Oprah's newfound success was now receiving national recognition, and she was ready for a change. About that time, the general manager of *A.M. Chicago* had viewed one of Oprah's talk show tapes. He was nothing more than stunned with her abilities. Before long, Oprah was hired to be the new host of *A.M. Chicago*.

Oprah's biggest challenge was the fact that *Donahue* was based in Chicago. Many critics wondered if Oprah could compete with Donahue. Encouraged to leave Baltimore by her best friend, Gayle King, Oprah took the plunge. The Chicago audience took an immediate liking to Oprah. So much so that she eventually beat *Donahue* in ratings.

Within 12 weeks, *A.M. Chicago* had more viewers than Donahue. Seven months later, her show was extended to one hour. She interviewed well-known celebrities such as Tom Selleck, Sally Field, Paul McCartney, and, her personal idol, Barbara Walters (Brands, 1999).

The producer of the show, Debbie DiMaio, explained Oprah's secret of success in the following manner:

> She's 100% percent the same off-camera as on. People like her because they can relate to her. She's got all the same problems— overweight, boyfriend troubles, she's been poor. So when people see her on television they can say, 'That's my friend Oprah.' (Raatma, 2001, p. 51)

Her forte, however, was interviewing the "average" person. She would get ordinary people to divulge their personal traumatic experiences. These conversations were almost therapeutic to Winfrey. It was during one of her ordinary interviews that she openly discussed her most horrifying personal experience…being molested by numerous relatives and friends. She said:

> I think it was on that day that, for the first time, I recognized that I was not to blame…It happened on the air, as so many things happen for me. It happened on the air in the middle of someone else's experience, and I thought I was going to have a break-down on television. (Brands, 1999, p. 298)

The Food Battle

Fear of failure was Oprah's greatest downfall. One way in which to deal with her mounting stress was food. Eating gave her comfort. Unfortunately, it also caused her to gain a great deal of weight…something she still has difficulty controlling. Her eating habits soon became out of control.

Oprah would binge diet and lose substantial weight. She would meet regularly with nutritionists and dieticians. This would work temporarily; but when the pressure began to mount again, the eating would start as well.

Due to a lawsuit hearing, Oprah was forced to tape her show from Texas for a period of time. Oprah spent many hours defending her actions in the courtroom. During her stay, she actually gained 11 pounds. She noted, "I was strategizing with lawyers at night. I couldn't help but eat pie" (Lowe, 1998, p. 111).

Acting

Oprah's passion for reading led her to the novel *The Color Purple*. When she learned that the book was being developed into a film, she approached one of the producers, Quincy Jones, to assist in some fashion. Mr. Jones was so impressed with her television talent that he asked her to play the part of Sofia, one of the main characters in the film. Steven Spielberg, the director of the film, agreed that Oprah was the appropriate person for the role.

Although movie critics gave the film mixed reviews, Oprah was quick to defend it. She stated, "It's about endurance, survival, faith, and ultimate triumph" (Raatma, 2001, p. 55). The film itself received eleven Academy Award nominations, and Oprah was nominated in the category of best supporting actress. Additionally, she was nominated for a Golden Globe Award. Unfortunately, no awards were ever secured; nonetheless, the nominations were very satisfying for the entire cast.

Taking Control of Her Empire

In 1985, Oprah's attorneys encouraged her to take full control of her television show. She could then syndicate the show by "renting" it to various stations. She subsequently purchased *A.M. Chicago* and renamed it to the *Oprah Winfrey Show*. She was the first woman in history to own and produce her own talk show (Raatma, 2001).

In 1986, she starred in another film, *Native Son*. This movie, too, did not do well in the theater; but Oprah received much recognition for her devoted work. The experience inspired Oprah so much that she decided to open her own production company...Harpo Entertainment Group. The name Harpo is Oprah spelled backward. Harpo Entertainment Group is divided between divisions: Harpo Production, Inc., Harpo Films, and Harpo Video, Inc. (Raatma, 2001).

This period in Oprah's life was a personal success as well. In 1986, she met her current boyfriend, Stedman Graham. Another personal success was her decision to complete her college degree. She contacted Tennessee State University and arranged to participate in a project that would allow her to earn her degree. To this day, she provides ten student scholarships to her Alma Mater. The scholarships are named in honor of her father.

Finally, in 1987, Oprah won the first of many Emmy Awards. She won the award for best talk show host. The *Oprah Winfrey Show* won the award for the best talk show (Raatma, 2001).

It's apparent that Oprah came a long way from her early days in Mississippi. She was able to tackle the obstacles that surrounded her. Her self-confidence and self-esteem were enhanced, and she created both a successful personal and professional life.

The Oprah Winfrey Show

Oprah Winfrey soon gained the reputation (and ratings) of being number one in the talk show business. She was able to sympathize *and empathize* with others in desperate need.

Perhaps, most importantly, she insisted on talking about serious people issues during a period when a lot of other talk shows had degenerated into "freak shows"... where oddball people talked about strange and often risqué behavior. Even when shows like *Jerry Springer* became immensely popular, she refused to change her format, and insisted that her show and her guests maintain a high moral level.

She suggested solutions to the various problems her shows revealed. She would recommend books for her guests and audiences to read. These books would soon become bestsellers. Consequently, the publishing companies suddenly began knocking on her door. They deluged her with books to read, review; and, most importantly, potentially endorse on her television program.

The Infamous Lawsuit

Oprah Winfrey was on the fast track to becoming the nation's first black billionaire. Like other successful business individuals, Oprah became a target for lawsuits. One lawsuit that created the most publicity was brought by a group of cattlemen claiming that the Winfrey show on mad-cow disease had resulted in multimillion-dollar damage to their industry as well as them as individuals.

The trial would eventually take place in Amarillo, Texas. Oprah decided she would testify on her own behalf. In an effort to not lose any valuable time, Winfrey took her show to Amarillo where locals waited in line to get tickets to the filming.

After spending long days in court and filming her show in the evening, Oprah finally was read the verdict: she won! The court decided that Oprah had the right to free expression. "Free speech not only lives," she noted, "it rocks!" (Brands, 1999, p. 302). Even the lawsuit never kept Oprah from practicing her right to speech.

Oxygen Media

Later in 1998, Oprah decided to try her hand at the Internet. She joined other producers in forming Oxygen Media. The project includes a women's cable-television network. This network is linked to Oxygen's online services, which include Oprah.com, ThriveOnline, and Moms Online.

The Classroom

Having the urge to test her skills at teaching, Oprah and her fiancée, Stedman Graham, agreed to team-teach a course at Northwestern University. The course is titled *Dynamics of Leadership*. Oprah began the first lecture by quickly involving the students. She asks each student for a synonym for leadership. Her point to this assignment: Everyone has a different idea of a leader.

Bill Dedman writes in his article titled "Professor Oprah, Preaching What She Practices" (*New York Times*, October 10, 1999) that Oprah described her success as coming from setting goals and from achieving them. She described the value of having an authentic leadership style that matched one's personality. Leaders must look inward, admit mistakes, and recognize their weaknesses.

Dedman interviews students in Winfrey's class. One student portrays Oprah as, "funny, down to earth, and extremely charismatic." The student continues:

> To some extent, Oprah's role is one of motivation, as an example of somebody who came from extremely humble beginnings and has built an empire. It's easier to believe in my possibilities when I'm hearing it from somebody who's built an amazing career from nothing but charisma and hard work. (Dedman, *New York Times,* October 10, 1999)

Clearly Oprah's hectic schedule constraints limit her ability to teach regularly. For now, she enjoys the opportunity.

O, The Oprah Magazine

In 2000, Oprah attempted to conquer yet another goal. She took on the position as magazine founder and editorial director of *O, The Oprah Magazine*. The magazine is published monthly and encourages readers to make the most out of life. It offers celebrity interviews, articles about health and nutrition, self-help columns, and much more.

As noted in Raatma (2001), Oprah described the magazine's purpose in the following manner:

> My hope is that this magazine will help you lead a more productive life, one in which you feel a sense of vitality, cooperation, harmony, balance and reverence within yourself and in your encounters. That doesn't mean living a life without frustration, anxieties and disappointments. It means understanding that your choices move you forward or hold you back. (p. 93)

After the first issue went on display to the public, Oprah still was not content with the magazine. Clemetson writes in her *Newsweek* article ("Oprah on *Oprah*," January 8, 2001) that Winfrey complained that the layouts were not lush enough and that the writing was not smart enough. She ordered several reshoots and revisions for the second edition. By the third issue, the editor-in-chief resigned. The employee stated, "It was like riding a rocket, and the only one who was prepared for it was Oprah because she's been riding it for years." Oprah was able to secure a new editor who, like herself, is a perfectionist.

Timeline of Awards, Honors, and Recognition

Oprah's skills and abilities have earned her many awards, honors, and recognition. The following timeline provided by Raatma (2001) represents some of the more significant honors:

1972: Wins Miss Black Nashville pageant and Miss Black Tennessee pageant; receives scholarship to Tennessee State University.

1973: Co-anchors evening and weekend news for WTVF-TV.

1976: Begins co-hosting local news at WJZ-TV in Baltimore.

1977: Begins co-hosting *People Are Talking* at WJZ-TV.

1984: Begins hosting *A.M. Chicago* at WLS-TV.

1985: Purchases *A.M. Chicago* and renames it the *Oprah Winfrey Show*; stars in *The Color Purple*.

1986: Nominated for a Golden Globe and an Academy Award for her role in *The Color Purple*; the *Oprah Winfrey Show* becomes nationally syndicated; forms Harpo Productions; stars in *Native Son*; meets Stedman Graham.

1987: Receives her degree from Tennessee State University; wins Daytime Emmys for best talk show and best talk-show host.

1988: Stars in and produces television miniseries "The Women of Brewster Place"; renovates huge Chicago building for Harpo Productions.

1991: Testifies about child abuse before a U.S. Senate committee.

1993: President Clinton signs the National Child Protection Act into law; stars in and produces *There Are No Children Here*.

1994: In the Kitchen with Rosie is published.

1996: Make the Connection: Ten Steps to a Better Body and a Better Personal Life is published; begins Oprah's Book Club; is sued by Texas cattle ranchers for her comments about beef; receives the George Foster Peabody Individual Achievement Award and the International Radio and Television Society's Gold Medal Award.

1997: Starts Oprah's Angel Network; stars in and produces *Before Women Had Wings*; produces the home video *Make the Connection*; is named *Newsweek* magazine's most important person in books and media.

1998: Wins Texas cattle ranchers' court case; stars in and produces *Beloved*; named one of the 100 most influential people of the twentieth century by *Time* magazine; joins other producers in launching Oxygen Media, Inc.; receives a lifetime achievement award from the National Academy of Television Arts and Sciences.

1999: Begins teaching with Stedman Graham at Northwestern University's J.L. Kellogg Graduate School of Management; receives the National Book Foundation's 50th Anniversary Gold Medal for the Oprah's Book Club contribution to books and authors.

2000: Launches *O, The Oprah Magazine.*

Leadership Traits

It's interesting that, while Oprah Winfrey was the victim of both racial and sexual discrimination in her youth, she has reached her success without attempting to capitalize on this discrimination and by exhibiting universal leadership traits that transcend her color and her sex. While some African-American leaders understandably use the discrimination that they have faced as a tool for gaining and maintaining media attention, Oprah Winfrey has never seemed to rely on any kind of assistance. Her leadership traits, as detailed by Landrum in *Profiles of Black Success* (1997), transcend all boundaries of sex and color. The descriptions below are condensations of the detailed character analysis included in *Profiles of Black Success* (1997, pp. 343-347).

Charisma: Winfrey is a charismatic woman with an irresistible charm for the millions of American viewers who have become loyal fans over the years. Her charismatic appeal is almost a therapeutic mechanism for those who watch her program. It's this charisma, more than any other single trait, that has made Oprah one of the most influential and wealthy women in America.

Competitiveness: The desire and the need to become number one is what drives Oprah Winfrey. Whatever she attempts to tackle...whether it be acting, hosting, or playing...she strives to be very good at. Her aggression and assertiveness drive her to success.

Confidence: Winfrey's mantra is "Uplift, encourage, empower!," and she does her best to live her life this way. She seemed to know, from a very early age, that she was destined for greatness. As a teenager, she wrote in her journal, "I will be famous!" While most people say, "I *want* to be or do such and such," Oprah characteristically says "I *will* be or do such and such." The difference in these two attitudes is confidence...and Oprah has confidence in abundance.

Passion and Drive: Like most natural leaders, Oprah is driven. As she told Larry King when he interviewed her on his show, she's driven "To reach somebody... I never did it for money. I'm convinced my television show is my calling in life. Everybody has a calling, and mine is TV."

Workaholic Tendency: Oprah is a classic workaholic. She finds satisfaction in doing a task well, and she never seems to allow time to be a factor in determining when the job is truly done well. She averages only about five hours of sleep per night, and she thus has more hours per day to devote to her work. She's a typical Type A person who always seems to achieve more...but that's primarily because she works harder and longer than the average person.

Independence: Oprah has always refused to bow to tradition, and has insisted on doing things her own way. She refuses to work from tight scripts, she consistently defies authority (without breaking any laws), and she seems to enjoy being the sort of maverick whom many of her viewers would like to be.

Perfectionist: Oprah is a demanding taskmaster who insists on the best efforts from herself and all of her employees. She is a true hands-on executive who reserves the exclusive right to accept or reject any changes in the format of her far-flung operations. In many ways, she is a control freak...but this insistence on control has served her well in her rise to the top of her profession.

Tenacity: Oprah Winfrey is a true survivor. In 1993, she won the Horatio Alger Award, a prestigious honor that is traditionally bestowed on people who best personify the "rags-to-riches" route to success. Early in her career, if things didn't go well, she simply changed her venue to suit her unique talents. Most leaders meet with failure of one kind or another before they finally achieve success...Oprah is no exception.

Vision: While different leaders often exhibit different attributes, the one attribute that seems to be shared by all successful men and women is "vision." Vision can be defined in many ways...and it obviously changes from occupation to occupation, but all leaders seem to have the knack of seeing the "big picture" and not becoming bogged down in details. Even though Oprah has perfectionist, controlling tendencies, no one has ever doubted her ability to see the big picture...and the big opportunity.

A Day with Oprah

Oprah Winfrey is a dedicated, die-hard professional. She is a perfectionist who expects the same from her staff. People who work for Oprah do so with extreme loyalty. They work long hours and put forth great sacrifice to keep up with Oprah's demands. One former producer noted the following, "People adore her. They give up their lives for her. People who work [at Harpo] get divorced, put off having kids, have no outside lives. Because everything, all your time and energy, is given to Oprah" (as cited in Raatma, 2001, p. 80).

Oprah is used to total control. She is a shrewd businesswoman who signs all checks in excess of $1,000 for her Harpo Entertainment Group. She has also been known to scrutinize the smaller checks that others on her staff have the authority to sign for. She attempts to bind all employees to strict, lifelong confidentiality agreements. She keeps a keen eye on her personal ventures as well. In the past, she barred the press from the course she taught with Stedman Graham at Northwestern University's business school. Students who chose to talk to reporters could face disciplinary action from the school (*Newsweek*, January 8, 2001).

Down-to-earth diva...control freak...silly...caring...perfectionist ...optimist. These are all words that accurately describe Oprah Winfrey. *Newsweek* Magazine (January 8, 2001) describes a typical day with Oprah:

It's Friday afternoon, and Oprah Winfrey is in an otherworldly state of calm. Her staff, however, is frantic. Nelson Mandela is about to arrive for a TV interview, and producers are rushing through set-checks, tightening security and prepping audience members. Behind the closed double doors to her Chicago office, Winfrey is plopped down in a cushiony armchair, a candle burning at her side, talking about the past year, when an assistant calls in a panic. Mr. Mandela is 30 minutes early, and Winfrey is still in her off-air gear—a baggy sweater and a well-worn pair of pants. "He'll just have to see me with no makeup on," says Winfrey, raking a hand through her unstyled hair. At least a little foundation and powder? The caller pleads. "Look," Winfrey replies before hanging up the phone, "he's seen a woman with no makeup on before." Her instincts are right. Mandela is charmed by the casual welcome.

Four days later, Winfrey is in perfectionist mode. Looking back at the December issue of her new magazine, *O*, she holds up the cover and winces. "Ooh, there's a mistake!" she says, pointing to the word "generosity," which she thinks should have bigger type. Annoyed with herself for not spotting it sooner, she grabs a stack of past issues and starts flipping. "Didn't like that." Flip. "Nope. Never got that right." Flip. Flip. Realizing that she's obsessing, she blows out a whoosh of breath and refocuses her energy on pages she likes. After several satisfied nods, she returns to the December issue and declares: "I love everything in this!" Then she turns a page, spots another imperceptible glitch and adds sheepishly: "Except this. We should have moved this."

Hours later, while teaching a business-school class at Northwestern University, Winfrey turns on her down-home charm. The course is called "The Dynamics of Leadership," and the night's topic—adapting strategies of the civil-rights movement to modern business—is heavy. But Winfrey knows how to keep the three-hour class moving. When guest speaker Coretta Scott King talks earnestly of her late husband's belief in service as the key to leadership, Winfrey raises her hand, stands and asks, "I mean, on your first date was [the Reverend King] just sitting up talking to you about service?" Laughter ripples through the classroom.

Clearly, as Winfrey's assets continue to grow at exponential rates, micromanaging will not be a feasible option for the multimillionaire. She will simply have to give up some amount of control in some areas. She'll probably do this very begrudgingly—but there will be no alternative.

Oprah's Ten Commandments

Millions of words have been written about Oprah and her many temperaments. Writers have dissected her as an actress, an entertainer, a counselor, a business leader, and as a female success in a male-dominated world. But in order to really delve into her complex persona, it's important to study what she thinks of herself, and what she views as her outlook on her success. We can gain some extremely valuable insight into her inner feelings from a set of 10 commandments that she says guide her success (Lowe, 1998, pp. 168-169). They include the following:

1. Don't live your life to please others.

2. Don't depend on forces outside yourself to get ahead.

3. Seek harmony and compassion in your business and personal life.

4. Get rid of the back-stabbers—surround yourself only with people who will lift you higher.

5. Be nice.

6. Rid yourself of your addictions—whether they be food, alcohol, drugs, or behavior habits.

7. Surround yourself with people who are as smart or smarter than yourself.

8. If money is your motivation, forget it.

9. Never hand over your power to someone else.

10. Be persistent in pursuing your dreams.

Oprah and the Future

Winfrey is a tireless businesswoman with endless energy. She is constantly working to accomplish her goals. She is a philanthropist who has donated millions to various charities. She is also an actress, television producer, CEO, and educator with a personal fortune estimated in excess of $800 million. She is obviously a very talented, very busy, very complex person. There is no question about the fact that she is a leader. But the thing she is most proud of is the fact that the American people relate to her, and consider her their good friend.

References

Brands, H.W. (1999). *Masters of enterprise.* New York: Simon & Schuster, Inc.

Branham, C. (1998). *Profiles of great African Americans.* Lincolnwood, IL: Publications International, Ltd.

Clemetson, L. (2001, January 8). Oprah on Oprah. *Newsweek,* 137, 38-44+

Dedman, B. (1999, October 10). Professor Oprah, preaching what she practices. *New York Times.*

Landrum, G. (1997). *Profiles of Black success.* Ahnerst, NY: Prometheus Books.

Lowe, J. (1998). *Oprah Winfrey speaks insight from the world's most influential voice.* New York: John Wiley & Sons, Inc.

Raatma, L. (2001). *Oprah Winfrey entertainer, producer, and businesswoman.* Chicago, IL: Ferguson Publishing Company.

A Final Thought...

Leadership is a phenomenon that has been studied for many centuries. Undoubtedly, it will continue to intrigue individuals into the foreseeable future. This fascination will possess scholars, academicians, and business executives to push forward seeking answers to such questions as, "What makes one a good leader?" "Is leadership innate or can it be learned?" "What characteristics are required to become a successful CEO?" While there doesn't appear to be a single definitive answer to these questions, many individuals have become better, more effective leaders in the pursuit of finding the answers.

There are only a handful of world-renowned leaders such as Jack Welch, Jeffrey Bezos, Michael Dell, and the like; but by studying these individuals and attempting to decipher their respective leadership qualities, one can develop and enhance his or her leadership skills and abilities and advance within any organization.

Index